THE PROPHET'S NOTEBOOK

By the same author
Springtime in the Church
Walking on Water
Another Way
The King Among Us
Riding the Storm

The Prophet's Notebook

BARRY KISSELL

KINGSWAY PUBLICATIONS
EASTBOURNE

First published 2002

ISBN 1 84291 002 7

Published by
KINGSWAY COMMUNICATIONS LTD
Lottbridge Drove, Eastbourne, BN23 6NT, England.
Email: books@kingsway.co.uk

Book design and production for the publishers by
Bookprint Creative Services, P.O. Box 827, BN21 3YJ, England.
Printed in Great Britain.

I dedicate this book to my eldest son Jonathan
for whose generation the time has come

Contents

Introduction to the Series

With many of my contemporaries, I have had the incredible privilege of being involved in three significant moves of the Holy Spirit.

As a student in the 1960s, studying theology mostly from an academic point of view, I could hardly believe it when, sitting in the college library one day revising for an examination, I started spontaneously to speak in tongues. Shortly afterwards I had an extraordinary revelation during which I heard the voice of God. The charismatic movement within the churches was such a great blessing to those who entered into it. This visitation of the Spirit transformed the life of the church in which I served and all the churches that welcomed his coming.

In the late 1970s I knew that there was going to come a new movement of the Spirit. I had heard the Lord say that it would be known as the 'Third Wave'. In our family this wave struck my wife Mary first. John Wimber prayed for her at a meeting in our church. She returned home on fire. The fire radiated from her for at least 24 hours. Its outworking has been seen in significant teaching, healing and counselling gifts. This has been equally true for the many others who were empowered in those days. If the charismatic movement was the rediscovery of the living Jesus and the gifts of his Spirit, then the Third Wave involved meeting with the anointed Jesus and the power of the Holy Spirit.

In the early 1990s a significant move of the Spirit happened in Toronto, Canada, and spread to other nations. Six months previously, on a hillside outside Shepton Mallet in Somerset, the Lord had shown me a vision in which I saw water flowing in every conceivable form. As I watched in wonder, he told me that he was going to refresh his church. What I subsequently saw happening was the Lord delivering people from bondages which had imprisoned them for years, even lifetimes. After the deliverance came a refreshing and incredible joy.

During three decades I have been based at one church and have experienced these moves of the Spirit within the same congregation. From St Andrew's, Chorleywood, I have travelled with Faith Sharing teams to over a thousand churches in 23 nations and have watched similar manifestations of the Spirit according to the particular season.

Over these years I have been in both large gatherings and small. I have seen the power of God falling upon countless numbers of people, anointing them to minister in God's church as apostles, prophets, evangelists, pastors and teachers. On many occasions I have heard the Lord ask me this same question: 'I have anointed them, but where are the mature?' By now these ministries should be active in all congregations of Spirit-filled churches.

During these different moves of God I have kept notebooks in which I jotted down what I believed to be significant revelations of God to me. These have included visions, dreams and words. It was from these notebooks that the idea for this series was born. Most of the authors would not claim to be theologians. Their expertise, if any, has been in taking note of truths from God which have helped them in developing their ministries as apostles, prophets, evangelists, pastors and teachers.

I sense that this present 'lull' of the Spirit is in its later stages. The next wave of the Spirit is already building significantly and will soon be breaking upon the churches. There will be fire in the cities and a great ingathering of people to the churches.

It is important that we take God's anointing and calling seriously. We need to be committed to seeking maturity in God's gifting on our lives. In the coming days all five of these ministries will be crucial in the equipping and leading of the churches. We pray that the insights of this series will encourage you on your way to maturity and fruitfulness in the kingdom of God.

Barry Kissell

Preface

This is not a theological tome on prophecy. It is first and foremost a notebook which reflects various aspects of prophecy that I have observed and noted over many years. I am sharing ways in which God has seemingly spoken to me, and through me to others. My aim in writing the notebook is twofold. First, I want to affirm and encourage all those who have stepped out and acted when they thought they heard the voice of God. Through what I have shared I want you to be able to say with confidence in your own situation, 'Yes, it was God who showed me that vision and gave me that word.' Second, I want what I have written to help equip and encourage a generation of prophetic people whose time has come.

In all my tentative prophetic steps, my human reference point has always been my wife, Mary, whose wisdom and insights have so often helped me to avoid making really big blunders.

I am grateful to Ali Herbert, my secretary and PA, for all the work she has done in preparing the manuscript. Her prophetic insights have enabled me to see more clearly.

I thank all those who attended the School for Prophets at St Andrew's, Chorleywood, and my new church St Mary's,

Bryanstone Square, London. You will never know the encouragement you have been as you graciously and humbly shared your prophetic insights.

I have always considered the artist to be a prophet to the culture. I thank my artist daughter Natasha for her insights and contribution, particularly in the chapter 'The Artist as the Prophet' which she wrote with me.

On this continuous prophetic journey I will always be indebted to Paul Cain and Bob Jones, whose revelations into our lives and those of our family have been truly remarkable and have affirmed to us again that God indeed speaks today.

Finally, I have written this book for those of you who know the prophetic calling. My hope is that you will allow the Lord to mature you and use you to free people from the insanity that has come upon this nation.

1

The Emerging Prophet

And afterwards,
I will pour out my Spirit on all people.
Your sons and daughters will prophesy,
your old men will dream dreams,
your young men will see visions.
(Joel 2:28)

God's plan for a prophetic people

God always intended his people to be a prophetic people. It was his plan that each person would hear his voice and be able to speak it out to others. At the giving of the law at Mount Sinai, however, the people blatantly rejected this. Scripture records that, after they had heard the voice of God as a community, a deputation came to Moses and said, 'Speak to us yourself and we will listen. But do not have God speak to us or we will die' (Exodus 20:19).

On another occasion Moses was finding the pressure of leadership more than he could bear, so he asked the Lord either to change the situation or to allow him to die. In reply the Lord told him to bring together 70 of Israel's recognized leaders so that he could anoint them also with his Spirit.

Obediently, Moses gathered the leaders in the Tent of Meeting. The Lord met with them all and took a portion of the Spirit that had rested on Moses and poured it out on each of them. Each of these leaders in the Tent then prophesied. While this was happening, back inside the camp, the Spirit unexpectedly rested upon two men named Eldad and Medad, and they too prophesied.

Joshua witnessed these men prophesying, became indignant and immediately reported to Moses exactly what had occurred. Moses answered him with a question, saying, 'Are you jealous for my sake? I wish that all the Lord's people were prophets and that the Lord would put his Spirit on them!' (Numbers 11:28). He was deliberately reaffirming God's original intention that they would be a prophetic people.

The prophetic ministry is linked directly with a person receiving the anointing of the Spirit. As Micah said when he compared himself with the false prophets of his day, 'But as for me, I am filled with power, with the Spirit of the Lord' (Micah 3:8). The prophets of Israel foretold a time when God would pour out his Spirit in an exceptional way. To the Jewish nation he said through Isaiah, 'For I will pour water on the thirsty land, and streams on the dry ground; I will pour out my Spirit on your offspring, and my blessing on your descendants' (Isaiah 44:3).

The universal outpouring

Through the prophet Joel, God extended this promise to include not only the people of Israel but also all other peoples. In the future there would be a universal outpouring of the Spirit, and this would once again make God's people a prophetic people.

Joel prophesied, 'And afterwards, I will pour out my

Spirit on all people. Your sons and daughters will prophesy, your old men will dream dreams, your young men will see visions' (Joel 2:28). Prophecy, dreams, visions: each of these manifestations of the Spirit's presence involves God communicating through revelation. Together they also speak of a maturing process, which we shall explore further later.

The all-inclusiveness of the promise is underlined when Joel states that even servants and women will receive the Spirit and prophesy (v. 29). In the culture of the time, these groups of people were considered to be of little value, yet they are specifically included here.

In the early days of the Christian faith, Paul wrote a letter to a fast-growing church in Corinth addressing some of their problems. This was a fellowship that was gifted by God in a variety of ways, but one area of abuse concerned the use of spiritual gifts. Having emphasized that love for others must motivate the exercising of all gifts, Paul writes, 'and eagerly desire spiritual gifts, especially the gift of prophecy' (1 Corinthians 14:1).

The context of this counsel is that of a church which has gathered to worship God. On such occasions any member could receive a prophetic gift to strengthen, encourage and comfort the congregation. Equally, there could be occasions when a believer was given a revelation into the life of an unbeliever. When he spoke this revelation publicly, the recipient would be shown 'the secrets of his heart', and he would 'fall down and worship God' (v. 25).

Having had the privilege of being on the staff of St Andrew's, Chorleywood, for 30 years, I have been able to watch the development of the prophetic ministry within a congregation. As at Corinth, there were many who prophesied occasionally. There were also four or five people who prophesied regularly and, as I listened to them over the decades, I described them as prophets. The messages they brought were often significant to the life of the church and changed the direction of our services. These particular individuals practised regularly what others did occasionally, and it became their ministry. It was part of their identity and a significant part of what they contributed to the body of Christ. All Christians are potential or actual prophets and need to seek the reality and outworking of this in their lives.

In this notebook I am not equating the Old Testament prophets with the emerging prophetic ministry today. (If you wish to explore the differences more deeply, see Wayne Grudem's thorough treatment of the subject in *The Gift of Prophecy*, published by Kingsway.) The prophets of Israel were uniquely appointed and anointed to their ministry in the same way as the kings, priests and judges were to theirs. The revelations they received were for the people of God and the nation – which was, of course, the same thing. The clarity of their revelation was such that what they spoke were the very words of God.

In contrast, the emerging prophetic ministry today is, in Paul's terms, 'imperfect'. He writes to the church in Corinth, 'We know in part and prophesy in part' (1 Corinthians 13:9). He likens what the prophet sees to looking into a mirror (v. 12). He can only see within the borders of that mirror, and he is receiving just a glimpse, not the whole picture.

What I am seeking to do in this book is to draw on principles and examples of hearing God which are timeless.

Hearing God's voice

On the morning of the 27th September 1971, Mary left the house to take our children to school and I went into my study to read the Scriptures and pray. As I opened the door I heard a friendly man's voice say, 'I will guide you.' This took me completely by surprise as there was no one in the room. I quickly searched the rest of the house, only to find it empty. Returning to my study, I sat quietly, realizing that it was the Lord. I had been a Christian for 12 years, and this was the first time I had heard the external, audible voice of God.

The previous evening we had been welcomed onto the staff of St Andrews, Chorleywood. Iain Roberts, a godly neurosurgeon and churchwarden, had taken me aside privately to say that prior to my coming he had been praying for me and felt the Lord had spoken to him about me through a specific scripture. He read to me from Deuteronomy 31:7–8, the word given by Moses to Joshua, who was to lead God's people into the Promised Land.

> Then Moses summoned Joshua and said to him in the presence of all Israel, 'Be strong and courageous, for you must go with this people into the land that the Lord swore to their forefathers to give them, and you must divide it among them as their inheritance. The Lord himself goes before you and will be with you; he will never leave you nor forsake you. Do not be afraid; do not be discouraged.'

Iain then said to me that this was to be God's calling on my life.

I never felt that this was some great and unique calling, because this is the call upon every Christian leader. Nonetheless, I did wonder how this would work itself out in my particular situation. The very next day, the Lord said audibly to me, 'I will guide you.' Thirty years later, having ministered in over a thousand churches in 23 nations, I can say that this has indeed been true for me.

The voice with which God spoke audibly to me in my study in 1971 was the same voice with which he spoke to Isaiah, Jeremiah and the prophets. God does not have two voices, although he can speak in every language known to humankind.

An emerging prophet will start to hear this voice of God, whether internally or externally. It can begin from a very early age, as it did with Samuel (see 1 Samuel 3:1ff). When he was just a child, his mother dedicated him to the ministry of the Lord and put him under the guardianship of Eli, the priest at Shiloh. Early one evening Samuel was lying in bed when he heard an audible voice call him by name. He thought it was Eli, and ran to where the priest lay, but Eli denied speaking and promptly sent him back to his bed. This happened twice more, until finally Eli realized that the boy was hearing the voice of God. He instructed Samuel to ask God to speak. The Lord then proceeded to reveal to this young boy all that he planned to do in the nation.

Often a calling at such a young age can be an overwhelming experience. It certainly was for Jeremiah (see Jeremiah 1:1ff). The voice of God told Jeremiah that even before his birth he had been chosen to be a prophet to the nations. Jeremiah protested that he was only a child and – on account of his age – questioned his suitability for such an onerous task. Isaiah seems to have had a similar experience. These young men were the forerunners of the young men and women who would prophesy when the Spirit was outpoured (see Joel 2:28).

In the Bible the prophetic gifting often passed down through families. We see this in the case of Asaph, Heman and Jeduthun and their respective sons (see 1 Chronicles 25:1ff) – whole families gifted prophetically for the leading of worship. Many of the Major

Prophets also came from prophetic families.

When Deborah led the nation against Jabin, the Canaanite king, she had the men of Issachar with her (see Judges 5:15). It was said that they were 'men ... who understood the times and knew what Israel should do – 200 chiefs, with all their relatives under their command' (1 Chronicles 12:32).

Then at Bethel, when Amos was challenged over his prophetic authenticity by Amaziah the priest, he replied, 'I was neither a prophet nor a prophet's son, but I was a shepherd and I also took care of sycamore-fig trees' (Amos 7:13). In this he implies that normally the prophetic gifting was passed down from father to son.

The 'fire' experience

The prophets in the Bible usually had a special encounter with the voice of God which launched them into their prophetic ministry. Some of the prophets also had to pass through a 'fire' experience. This often involved a brush with death, as in the case of Jeremiah. Because of the words he spoke concerning God's judgement by the Babylonians, an opposition group had him lowered into a cistern where he sank into the mud. It was only the intervention of King Zedekiah that saved him from death (see Jeremiah 38).

One evening Mary and I invited Paul Cain to supper. Paul is an American from Kansas City, and a very mature and experienced prophet of God. During the meal he told us of several occasions when he found himself in a situation in which he thought he was going to die. Little did I know at the time that I was to go through a similar life-threatening experience, described in detail in my book *Riding the Storm*. Such experiences put the prophet at the ultimate edge of existence, standing between this life and the life to come. I have found that my own near-death experience and subsequent sufferings have given me a sharper focus when seeking to understand the ways of the Spirit.

Maturing the prophet

There is an identifiable process by which God raises up the emerging prophet. Moses told the Israelites that God would 'raise up for you a prophet like me from among your own brothers' (Deuteronomy 18:15). This implies a maturing process, as does Joel's prophecy. 'Sons and daughters will prophesy' – this is simply to hear the voice of God and speak it. 'Old men will dream dreams' – the interpretation of dreams involves the understanding of symbols and signs. 'Young men will see visions' – this is to understand the meaning of pictures and impressions needing greater insight.

The Lord seeks to mature his prophets in a number of ways. These often involve subjecting them to difficult situations which necessitate total and unflinching faith in God. Ezekiel's wife was taken away; Jonah was tossed into the sea; Hosea had to marry a prostitute; Elijah fell under the death sentence of Jezebel; Amos was rejected and ridiculed by the establishment in Samaria; Daniel was thrown into the lions' den. The reality is that, if God does not resolve the situation, then all is hopeless.

In the maturing process God teaches the prophet to know his voice, to receive revelation and to have a quality of life that reflects the presence of God. Jesus the Good Shepherd says, 'The sheep listen to his voice. He calls his own sheep by name and leads them out. When he has brought out all his own, he goes on ahead of them,

and his sheep follow him because they know his voice'
(John 10:3–4).

Specific signs

For the prophet, the Word of God and the Spirit of God
flow into each other. The prophets were led by the Spirit to
take action in certain circumstances, and these directional
words allowed the prophet to step out in faith and in so
doing to fulfil the word of God.

On one occasion the Lord said to Isaiah, 'Go out, you
and your son Shear-Jashub, to meet Ahaz at the end of the
aqueduct of the Upper Pool, on the road to the
Washerman's Field' (Isaiah 7:3). It was here that he was to
meet the king and deliver a message that the Lord had
given him. This revelation is very specific.

On another occasion, the young evangelist Philip was
conducting meetings in Samaria (see Acts 8). At the height
of his evangelistic effectiveness, he was told by an angel of
the Lord, 'Go south to the road – the desert road – that
goes down from Jerusalem to Gaza' (v. 26). It was only as
he was obedient to this puzzling revelation that further
instructions were given. As he stood by the roadside, he
saw a chariot carrying a man who was returning home
after worshipping in Jerusalem. This man turned out to be
the Ethiopian chancellor and, as Philip watched him
approach, the Holy Spirit said to him, 'Go to that chariot
and stay near it' (v. 29). Philip was once again obedient to
this instruction and was then able to speak with the official
about Jesus and eventually lead him to faith.

The sensitive heart

With the releasing of the prophetic gifting, the Spirit of

God starts to operate on the prophet's heart in a number of ways. On one occasion Jesus asked his disciples who people thought he was (see Matthew 16:13ff). The variety of replies – some thought he was Jeremiah or another of the prophets, some John the Baptist, some Elijah – gives a profound insight into Jesus' prophetic heart. Jeremiah, for example, was known as the 'weeping' prophet, because he felt the pain of what was going to happen to a people who largely rejected the words of the Lord. Such sensitivity is what the Lord seeks to create in the heart of every emerging prophet.

Paul Cain once came to speak at a conference for leaders at St Andrew's, Chorleywood. He was due to speak in the session after lunch. When the time came he stood up, mumbled a few things, and sat down. That evening over a meal, I tentatively asked him if he was planning to speak at the meeting later in the evening, and this led to a discussion of what had happened in the afternoon. Paul explained that when he rose to speak he was met by waves of cynicism, unbelief and what he sensed was a mocking spirit. The inner pain this caused was such that he was unable to share the word that he felt the Lord had given him for the leaders. Emerging prophets will start to feel the pain in unknown people and situations and, if speaking, will also begin to perceive how the group is reacting to them and to the message they are bringing.

Other people thought that Jesus was John the Baptist come back to life. John was courageous and faced situations head on. He told the king that committing adultery with his brother's wife was wrong in the sight of God, and he confronted the Pharisees directly with their hypocritical ways. Others thought Jesus was Elijah, whose coming was foretold by Malachi (4:5). Elijah was above all a man of faith, a miracle-worker and a 'man of the Spirit', the Spirit at times physically transporting him away.

God is seeking to create a sensitive, courageous, faith-filled heart within his prophets.

In the desert

The emerging prophet will experience a growing desire to be alone with the Lord. It is no coincidence that many of the prophets of Israel spent years in the desert before they started to bring the word of God to the people. Moses spent many years alone in the desert tending the flock of his father-in-law Jethro, and it was here that God started to speak with him through vision and word. John the Baptist spent many formative years in the desert before he began his national ministry, and that ministry did not happen until 'the word of God came to [him] in the desert' (Luke 3:2). The emerging prophet will discover a strong need to retreat into those places symbolized by the desert.

At The Grail, a Roman Catholic community in Middlesex which I visited for many years, I was given the use of a *poustinia*, a small hut in the grounds containing only a table, chair and bed. It was my custom to arrive at eight in the morning and leave late in the afternoon. The objective of my visit was to make that place my desert and to retreat into the stillness, away from people and responsibilities. Initially I found this the hardest part of my spiritual pilgrimage, yet I wanted so much to do it, and I had a deep desire to be alone with God. Nevertheless, my expectations of a telephone-style conversation with God never materialized.

I have come to see that the key is just to spend time in the presence of God. Jeremiah was questioning the authenticity of some prophets, and he asked this question: 'But which of them has stood in the council of the Lord to see or to hear his word?' (Jeremiah 23:18)

Changing times

The emerging prophet will learn that God does nothing
without revealing his plans. If you are watching and listening, you will see the end of the old and catch glimpses of
the new thing that God intends to do. Once the new move
of God has started, it will usher in a new season of the
Spirit. As Solomon so poignantly puts it, 'There is a time
for everything, and a season for every activity under
heaven' (Ecclesiastes 3:1).

This is the time to be looking for the opportunity to prepare the church for the season you are beginning to see.
From the earliest days of prophetic ministry in the church,
this has always been the case. In the spring of AD 70, Titus
the Roman general laid siege to Jerusalem. The historian
Eusebius records that many of the Christian community
escaped to Pella, which was one of the cities in the
Decapolis. They escaped because the prophets had seen
that the church was entering a time of persecution and so
had warned the leaders of the church in Jerusalem.

Then there was the occasion when some prophets came
down from Jerusalem to Antioch. One of them was called
Agabus, and he predicted that a severe famine would
engulf the whole Roman Empire (see Acts 11:27ff). This
was going to be a difficult season for the church, but, having been forewarned, they were able to make provision.

There will be other times when the church will experience what Peter refers to as 'times of refreshing . . . from
the Lord' (Acts 3:19). These special seasons of the Spirit can
be likened to a wave of the sea. It builds, breaks and then
runs its course. Before it rebuilds again there is a period
that can be described as a 'lull'. It is during this time that
the prophets need to withdraw. David describes this with-
drawal in Psalm 103: 'The Lord . . . satisfies your desires

with good things so that your youth is renewed like the eagle's' (v. 5). Each year the eagle withdraws and undergoes a gradual moulting process, which prepares it for the new year. This is a time when the eagle discards the past and waits to receive a new plumage for the future. During this process it is most vulnerable to attack from predators. Similarly, for the emerging prophet this can be quite an unsettling and difficult time.

If the 'lull' is a vulnerable time for the emerging prophet, it is equally so for the church. Indeed, it can be the most dangerous time for the church. Since nothing seems to be happening, the leadership can be tempted to try to *create* new life. This may happen in a number of ways. Often an old activity which has long outgrown its usefulness is renovated and presented to the congregation as the 'new thing' God is intending to do. The home group becomes the 'cell'; the fellowship group becomes the 'area congregation' or 'local small church'. What the members do together is revamped in the hope that new life will be created in the reshuffle.

During the lull, leaders will also hear about what God is doing in other nations and will often go and see for themselves. They will return with the literature, videos and courses associated with that particular move of the Spirit. Their enthusiasm will excite a group within their congregation as they share how this new programme will herald in the new thing that God intends to do among them. It is not to be, however, because it is not the season.

The greatest danger to the church during the lull can come when the time is filled with man-made ideas and imported programmes. These can become very time consuming and exhausting. The manufactured ideas can so embrace a church that when the new season of the Spirit does come, the church is far too busy to take seriously what God is actually doing.

During the lull, emerging prophets must keep their council until they start to see through dreams, visions and the whispered word what is really on the heart of God for the new season.

The watchman

The word for 'council' in Hebrew is *sod*, which translates literally as 'consulting room'. God consults with a heavenly council, and he invites the prophet to be part of this process. In the heavenly context the Lord is having consultations with heavenly beings and the prophet is invited to hear their deliberations. Jeremiah says of the false prophets, 'If they had stood in my *sod* (i.e. my council) they would have proclaimed my words to my people.' Amos in a famous passage states, 'Surely the Sovereign Lord does nothing without revealing his *sod* (i.e. what he has planned and decided) to his servants the prophets.'

In 1 Kings Micaiah the prophet 'saw the Lord sitting on his throne with all the host of heaven standing round him on his right and on his left. And the Lord said, "Who will entice Ahab into attacking Ramoth Gilead . . . ?"' (1 Kings 22:19–20). In a similar way, Isaiah heard the questioning call of God and volunteered to be involved (see Isaiah 6:8). God does not act in isolation – the prophets are always informed. We must consciously put ourselves in a place where God can reveal to us something of his plans, and this means maintaining vigilance, watching and waiting on God.

It is in the desert that the emerging prophet learns to become the Lord's watchman. Hosea writes, 'The prophet, along with my God, is the watchman over Ephraim' (Hosea 9:8). When the Lord called Ezekiel, it was to be a 'watchman' for the house of Israel (Ezekiel 3:17; 33:7).

In the culture of the time, the watchmen were posted on the city walls to report on everything that was approaching the city. At times this would be an approaching enemy. Recently in our church, four prophets wrote independently to the leadership with a word of warning. They had not discussed with each other what they had written, but in meaning the words were very similar. They had been quietly watching alone from the city walls and had reported back what they saw.

On other occasions, the Lord may show the watchman the blessing that he is planning to pour upon his people. God has shown me his blessings a number of times and I have spoken and written about them before they have happened, as have many other prophetic people. This was certainly the case with the outpouring that was known as the 'Third Wave', and later with the 'Toronto Blessing'. The Lord showed me in word and vision both of these moves of the Spirit before they came to pass.

Many emerging prophets will start to become burdened to pray and intercede for people, churches and nations. This type of intercession will be different from ordinary prayer, because it springs directly from those things that God has revealed. A helpful example of this is Habukkuk's prayer as recorded in chapter 3 of his prophecy.

In the spiritual battle the emerging prophet is the devil's key target. If he can take the prophet out, if he can remove the watchman, then the church has lost its eyes and ears. At times the attacks will be vicious and seemingly unending. The devil attacked Jesus before he started his public prophetic ministry. He came to him in the desert when he was at his most vulnerable. A six-week fast had taken its physical and emotional toll. The initial attacks centred on the prophetic word which Jesus heard at his baptism. His

Father had affirmed him in the words, 'You are my Son, whom I love; with you I am well pleased' (Luke 3:21). The devil cast doubts on this. Jesus was also tempted to misuse spiritual power to fulfil his needs for food and self-affirmation. He was told lies, he heard Scripture being misused, and he was offered a way out that bypassed the cross.

The receiving of accurate revelation from God will open doors which will give emerging prophets access to the things that motivate the culture into which they speak. These will include opportunities to receive money, to have immoral relationships and to use revelatory information to manipulate people. Although Jesus could not stop himself hearing the words the devil spoke to him, he maintained his integrity by dismissing what he heard and committing himself to the truth of the words that his Father had already spoken.

Learning from the Bible

Prophets fill themselves with the word of God. This is the word which has already been revealed and is recorded in the Scriptures. When emerging prophets ask me where to start learning about the ways of God, I always refer them to the Minor Prophets. These twelve books start with Hosea and end with Malachi. I suggest they read through them asking the question, 'In what ways do these men receive the word of God?' These insights need to be noted, and we shall be looking at my own conclusions throughout this book. When they have worked through these books a number of times, I suggest they go on to read the Major Prophets, working systematically through Isaiah, Jeremiah and Ezekiel, again asking the same question. Finally I recommend that they go through the historical books and then into the New Testament, especially the

Acts of the Apostles and Paul's first letter to the Christians in Corinth.

The way in which God has revealed himself in the past, as recorded in the Bible, is the benchmark by which all present revelation is to be judged. God will not show his prophets anything contrary to that which has already been revealed.

The prophets quote and allude to words that God has spoken in the past. These words were originally spoken into a historical situation, but they can be prophetic once again when they are applied to a current situation.

Identifying with the word

Emerging prophets will start to feel a strong sense of identification both with the word they have received and with the people to whom they must deliver it. Micah the prophet received a disturbing revelation concerning the coming judgement of God on the northern city of Samaria and the southern city of Jerusalem. Total devastation was to come upon the cities and people (Micah 1:3ff). Micah responded in this way: 'Because of this I will weep and wail; I will go about barefoot and naked. I will howl like a jackal and moan like an owl' (1:8). In a similar situation Jeremiah reflects his own identification with the nation in this way: 'Since my people are crushed, I am crushed; I mourn, and horror grips me' (Jeremiah 8:21). The word always touched the prophet first, as he felt himself to be part of the nation on whom God was bringing judgement. Jesus the prophet did a similar thing: although sinless himself, with his baptism he completely identified with the sin of the people.

Emerging prophets may also discover that they have a preaching gift. As this matures, they will find themselves bringing prophetic sermons to the congregation. As with the gift of prophecy, however, it will be the community to which they belong that will confirm this gifting.

When I was travelling with the Faith Sharing teams, we were invited to lead a conference for a group of churches in an area of Stoke-on-Trent. This was during the season of the Spirit known as the 'Third Wave'. On the team was a young woman who was growing in the prophetic ministry but had never preached publicly. As I prepared for the conference, I felt that she should give one of the major talks of the weekend. At a team meeting before we went, I asked her whether she would consider doing this. Her initial reaction was one of total surprise, but she agreed to seek God to see whether he had a word for her to bring.

On the morning of the conference the organizers met with me and discussed how they should introduce me. I said that I would not be speaking – one of the young women on our team would take on that role. You could have heard a pin drop!

Mary stood tentatively behind the lectern at the front of a large, packed church. She read from Isaiah 43. As she finished, I sensed a charge like electricity come upon the gathering. People were motionless, hanging on her every word. It was as if the word spoken 2,700 years ago through the prophet Isaiah was being spoken for the first time, through a young woman.

After a general introduction she came to her theme: 'Forget the former things; do not dwell on the past. See, I am doing a new thing! Now it springs up; do you not perceive it? I am making a way in the desert and streams in the wasteland' (Isaiah 43:18–19).

She preached a powerful prophetic sermon. Isaiah had spoken this word originally because it was God's intention to bring his people back from exile in Babylon, and so they were not to dwell on what God had done in the past. The words referred to the events surrounding the Exodus when God made a path through the sea. Now, in the present, God was doing a new thing, making a way through the desert. The obvious application was that the new way was the Third Wave, which at that time was breaking upon the churches.

A past prophet's word had become a present prophet's word through a young woman preacher. The word spoken 2,700 years ago was again prophetic. It revealed God's intention in the present situation.

There will be times when the Lord will also ask the prophet to do something, to take some action, as part of a prophetic sermon. On one occasion I was preparing to speak at a celebration at our church. It was a special evening, because a hundred or more people who had attended an Alpha weekend were going to be present. I took as my theme the need to have faith in Jesus. I had many illustrations from both the Gospels and the present time.

While I was preparing, I heard the Lord say to me, 'Buy a 40-foot rope and throw it over the gathering, as a cowboy would lasso a horse.' I duly bought a 40-foot rope and spent some time in our street practising how to throw it, with varying degrees of accuracy. It was only a small street, and my activities caused a certain amount of interest. The local children entered into the fun with great enthusiasm, and their parents watched with some incredulity from behind their lace curtains!

It was not until I started to preach that I realized the full implication of that rope. I found myself saying that our faith in Jesus was like taking hold of a rope which had been thrown to us. This rope, although present with us, also disappeared into the distance (see Hebrews 6:19). At that moment I threw the rope over the people. The practice sessions had been fruitful and the 40-foot length of nylon disappeared into the crowd. I invited anyone who would like to put his or her faith in Jesus to take hold of the rope. Many people did, and for some it was the start of their Christian lives.

A common reason for a prophet not being heard or not receiving a response is that he or she is speaking out of unresolved emotions. The revelation that the prophet brings may well be true, but the anger or resentment with which it is spoken makes it a message people are simply unable to receive and accept. We shall move on now to look at how the Lord facilitates the healing of his prophets.

2

The Prophet's Healing

> The Spirit of the Sovereign Lord is on me,
> because the Lord has anointed me
> to preach good news to the poor.
> He has sent me to bind up the broken-hearted,
> to proclaim freedom for the captives
> and release from darkness for the prisoners.
> (Isaiah 61:1)

God wants to mature the emerging prophet in two areas simultaneously – in the gift that has been given and in the heart. It is from the heart that the prophet speaks the word of God, so if the heart is full of bitterness or resentment, then the word spoken will be affected and the people will be unable to receive it. The revelation may well be true, but because of the way it is spoken – and the spirit in which it is given – people are unable to hear it.

Rejection of the prophet

Prophets will often find themselves subtly persecuted and sidelined by those who are wedded to the traditions of their particular brand of Christianity. Their inherited interpretations of Scripture and the ways in which God speaks override everything they hear. Others may have compromised themselves spiritually and morally, and find the prophetic word unacceptable.

Summarizing the people's reaction to the prophet's function in his day, Hosea wrote, 'The prophet is considered a fool, the inspired man a maniac. The prophet, along with my God, is the watchman over Ephraim, yet snares await him on all his paths, and hostility in the house of his God' (Hosea 9:7–8).

Jesus also spoke of how people responded to prophets: 'O Jerusalem, Jerusalem, you who kill the prophets and stone those sent to you' (Matthew 23:37). He referred to a time after his own death, saying, 'I am sending you prophets and wise men and teachers. Some of them you will kill and crucify' (23:34). Similarly, when the members of the Sanhedrin were trying him for blasphemy, Stephen, a young church leader, asked, 'Was there ever a prophet your fathers did not persecute?' (Acts 7:52).

The history of the prophetic ministry is one of rejection, and the emerging prophet will always have to live and deal with that factor. Nonetheless, it is important that the reason for the persecution and rejection is the word of God, and not our unresolved lives.

A broken and vulnerable people

Often the Lord anoints into the prophetic ministry very rejected and broken people. The reason for this is that their sufferings have made them sensitive and have given them an ability to both see and hear the word of God. This vulnerability, however, also leaves them open to seeking comfort in the wrong way and makes them prey to the attacks of the enemy. It is important, therefore, that the emerging prophet constantly seeks the healing and transforming power of Jesus and his Spirit.

The prophet speaks from the heart. Consequently it is essential that the heart is in an ongoing healing relationship with God. Jesus' 'ministry manifesto' was based on the prophecy of Isaiah as recorded in chapter 61 of his book: 'The Spirit of the Sovereign Lord is on me . . . to preach good news to the poor. He has sent me to bind up the broken-hearted' (v. 1).

The term 'heart' in Scripture describes who we are, what makes us unique, our personality. The term 'broken-hearted' encompasses every fracturing of our personality: our minds, emotions, spirits, souls and bodies can all be crippled as the result of a broken heart.

What others deny us

Hearts can be broken in a variety of ways. It can happen through what others deny us. It would seem from Scripture that God ordained a charter for children which could be summarized in this way: 'A child has the right to be loved, to feel safe and protected within his or her own family, to receive from both father and mother all that is needed for physical, emotional and spiritual maturity.'

Ideally, a loving and committed relationship between father and mother will provide stability and protection for the child. The father is the leader of the family that he protects and provides for, and in the way he conducts his life and relationships he models for his children what it means to be a man. Meanwhile, the mother's bonding love and intuition provide comfort and healing for the child, and she models what it means to be a woman.

Since the 1960s, Western society has challenged God's plan for the family, and this has created a broken-hearted and addicted generation. For many young people the separation of their parents and the subsequent breakdown of their families has caused great pain in their hearts. Having to deal with foster parents or their own parent's new partner has been equally traumatic. For a growing number the pain is so great that the only way it can be softened is through alcohol or drug abuse. Many emerging prophets are from this generation.

Marriage breakdown

Children's hearts can be broken through the failure of their parents' marriage. Often children blame themselves for the break-up, and suffer deep feelings of rejection and insecurity. In one family I know of, the parents separated and the two daughters had to choose with which parent they were going to live. The separation lasted for some years, after which, happily, there was reconciliation. The mother, however, would have nothing at all to do with the daughter who had chosen to live with her father. This reached a sad climax on the day of the daughter's wedding, when her mother publicly rejected her.

Similarly, a young man I knew was unable to maintain close relationships. When he was three years old, his father had walked out of the family home, although the young man remembered having a close and loving relationship with him before that time. He was never again to see his father, who committed suicide some years later.

Parental rejection

A child's heart can be broken through the rejection of a parent. This feeling of parental rejection is one of the deepest emotions that many emerging prophets may have to face. We were born into a family where God intended us to be welcomed and loved unconditionally, and therefore the experience of rejection can be devastating.

Rejection is like a deep taproot, which grows down into the very centre of our lives. Once this root starts to grow, then every other rejection, however small or irrational, acts like a shot of fertilizer. It stimulates growth and the root reaches even deeper into our emotions.

The ultimate rejection is for a child – for whatever reason – to be given away for adoption. Or a child could be the replacement in a family for a brother or sister who died. In her loss and grief, the mother may decide to withhold her love from the new baby, from fear of losing another child in the same way.

Sometimes, for reasons no one else may understand, parents can feel that a particular child does not fit into their family, and as a result the child can grow up feeling unloved and unaccepted as a family member. Over the years those feelings of rejection are compounded.

What others do to us

Hearts can also be broken through things that other people do to us. In this troubled generation, one of the major problems is abuse. It can take many different forms. Emotional abuse, for example, can happen simply through a parent rigidly controlling every aspect of their child's life.

A woman I once met had sought counselling for 18 years and had a severe eating disorder which caused her to make herself sick every time she ate. In a vision I saw a perfectly dressed little girl. Her hair was in ringlets, she wore a blue satin dress with puffed sleeves and long white socks, and her shoes were shining black patent leather. I spoke out what I was seeing, and the woman acknowledged that it was a description of her as a young child. The picture immediately made her agitated, because it reminded her of how her mother had controlled and directed every aspect of her life. As a result of this control, she had come to feel that it was impossible for her to please anyone in anything she did.

Constant physical abuse creates in the heart a great fear of punishment and retribution. This was the case with a young man who was regularly beaten senseless by his father and then locked in a dark cellar for many hours at a time. It was also the case with a young Frenchwoman whose father beat her every day. She recalled that after the beatings she would always climb under her bed to seek solace. Both of these young people were very prophetic, but were unable to exercise their gifting properly because of the unresolved trauma in their hearts.

Sexual abuse is pandemic in our culture. A young woman in her twenties had been abused over a long period of time. She blamed herself, and always felt unclean. The memories of certain instances continually tormented her. Although the abuse was in the past, she still suffered much in the present. Often, as she walked down the street, men she had never met would walk up to her and say disgusting or suggestive things. In this extreme case of trauma, an unclean spirit had attached itself to her. Those with similar unclean spirits had recognized a comparable uncleanness.

I have noticed that the abused often attract abuse, the bullied attract the bully, those who are blamed attract blame, and the emotionally controlled attract controlling people. These negative and destructive experiences all work against the emerging prophet.

What others say to us

Words have an exceptional power over those who hear them spoken. Words spoken over us in anger or ignorance can not only direct our subsequent thinking and actions but can also break our heart. Hearts can be broken through what others say to us.

The writer of Proverbs says, 'The tongue has the power of life and death' (Proverbs 18:21), and, 'Reckless words pierce like a sword' (12:18), and, 'A deceitful tongue crushes the spirit' (15:4).

I spoke with two emerging prophets whose great struggle was in this area. One was a man who was struggling with an abnormal lack of confidence. He was the last child of a large family. Ever since he could remember, his mother had introduced him to strangers in this way: 'This is George. He was our mistake.' She meant nothing particularly negative by this – simply that she and her husband had thought that their family was complete, and then unexpectedly a little boy had been born. Nonetheless, this consistently repeated statement had moulded George's life. In his marriage, with his young children and at work, he always thought that he was an unwelcome presence.

The other was a young woman in great distress. On the evening we met she had broken off her engagement to a young man with whom she was much in love. The breakup was an irrational and unwanted action, but as we talked it transpired that ever since she was a little girl, her mother had said to her periodically, 'You'll never marry.' These words had taken root in her life, and when marriage was imminent she was unable to proceed with it. Although she was starting to receive prophetic dreams, she was unable to embrace the prophetic gift completely because she felt unworthy.

Sometimes when people are hurt by words, they make oaths such as, 'I'll never forgive . . .' or, 'I'll never trust men/women again.' Jesus says that the devil is the source of such oaths (see Matthew 5:33) and that people who speak these oaths become spiritually bound in their hearts.

I was once asked by a team member to join her in praying over a lady. The lady in question had asked for prayer for her barrenness. She had been married for a number of years and had been unable to conceive. After tests, the doctors had said that there was no reason why she and her husband had not conceived. While she was being prayed with, the lady behaved very strangely. She fell to the ground and thrashed about in an agitated state. I talked with her, and she recounted to me her sadness at not being able to have children.

When I asked about her life prior to marriage, she said she had spent ten years or more in a convent as a nun. She had met a local builder and fallen in love, and this had led to her leaving the convent and getting married. Before the marriage her husband had been a wealthy builder in the local community, but afterwards the business had collapsed and was struggling to survive. As we spoke, the question of oaths came to my mind and I asked her what oaths she had taken. As a nun, she said, she had promised obedience, chastity and poverty. I suddenly saw why the business had failed and why they had been unable to have children. What she had sworn had become a reality. It was only after she was led to renounce the oath and was set free in Jesus' name that the oath lost its power.

What others expect of us

Hearts can be broken through what others expect of us. I once sought to help a young couple whose marriage was under great strain. The young wife's father had desperately wanted a boy, and he had been very disappointed with his baby daughter's arrival. She had sensed this from her earliest days and had adopted masculine ways, dressing and acting like a boy. Such confusion as to her real identity caused a crisis in her life and made her suppress her feminine side, which in turn made it difficult for her to form close relationships. The whole episode had broken her heart and destroyed her self-confidence.

Hearts can be broken through circumstances over which we have no control. In certain situations, this can give rise to severe panic attacks. A boy of twelve came to me with his mother to talk over his situation. Since he was a baby he had woken every night at 2 a.m. and had lain in bed screaming. His parents always rushed to be with him, but he was in a trance-like state and was not conscious of them being there. After a while he would calm down and go back to sleep. As they shared this with me, I heard the Lord say, 'It's grief.' It transpired that at his birth, the boy's mother had nearly died. Before she had even held him, the nursing staff had rushed him away and it was not until some days later that she had recovered enough to hold him. This had led him to experience a severe separation anxiety.

Dealing with wrong choices

Hearts can also be broken through wrong spiritual and moral choices. This is sin. Our hearts can be broken because of our own bad choices, but also because of the consequences of other people's bad choices.

It is important that the emerging prophet always seeks the healing and transforming power of Jesus and his Spirit. That means dealing with all sin in our lives. John, writing in his first epistle, makes this statement: 'If we claim to be without sin, we deceive ourselves and the truth is not in us. If we confess our sins, [God] is faithful and just and will forgive us our sins and purify us from all unrighteousness' (1 John 1:8–9).

We all sin, but it is vital that we turn to God and confess those things we have done against him. This will also, at times, necessitate us forgiving people we feel have hurt us by their words or attitudes. We are called to be a forgiven and forgiving people.

Binding up the brokenness

It is so often the unresolved emotions of the heart that cripple our ministry and hinder people from receiving what God has given us to speak. It is Jesus' intention to bind up and heal the brokenness within our hearts, and he will do this when we continue to seek him in our prayers. When he raises issues with us, it is important that we pursue them with him – even though this may mean that we have to face things we have avoided, suppressed, or even denied.

We have all experienced things – both major and minor events – that have cut or bruised our hearts. Once the Lord has brought such an experience into our conscious mind, then we need first to go over the situation as we remember it. It may be helpful to write everything down, or to seek a friend with whom we can discuss the incident.

A young woman who had seen her child killed in an accident had lived in denial of the event for seven years. After the funeral she had put all her son's clothes and photographs in a drawer which she had locked and never opened. To help her face the situation, I asked her to bring a photograph of her son to show me, so that we could talk about him together. This was a traumatic time, but afterwards I was able to put the power of the cross of Jesus between her and all that she had seen and experienced. The power of grief that had invaded her was finally broken.

Once we start to seek the Lord in this way, he will gradually work through our lives and we shall start to hear his voice. This is a vital message for the emerging prophet. If you have an unresolved background, such as I have discussed in this chapter, you run a double risk: you may speak out in an aggressive, judgemental way which will prevent other people from receiving your prophetic word, or you may turn in on yourself and become self-absorbed, bearing a 'martyr's crown'. God can heal your brokenness and release you into your full gifting. I am not implying, incidentally, that there is any deeper link between having a broken heart and being prophetic. Nonetheless, many prophetic people I know have come through much personal suffering.

3

The Dreamer

> When a prophet of the Lord is among you,
> I reveal myself to him in visions,
> I speak to him in dreams.
> (Numbers 12:6)

To dream is natural to all of us, but prophets may dream in quite a different way. Often dreams are mechanisms that enable us to resolve the anxieties of the day. As the 'Teacher of Ecclesiastes' records, 'A dream comes when there are many cares' (Ecclesiastes 5:3). Dreams such as these, however, often make no sense at all and are usually simply a collection of unrelated images. On the other hand, 'significant dreams', as we shall call them, are very different from these 'anxiety dreams', and are often film-like, vivid and remembered in detail on waking.

Significant, God-given dreams are inspired by the Holy Spirit and fulfil his kingdom purposes. Job writes, 'For God does speak – now one way, now another – though man may not perceive it. In a dream, in a vision of the night . . .' (Job 33:14–15). Here Job is stating something that is generally true for believers and non-believers alike, but receiving God-inspired dreams is a common experience for the emerging prophet.

As the Lord said to Moses and his brother and sister, 'When a prophet of the Lord is among you, I reveal myself to him in visions, I speak to him in dreams' (Numbers 12:6). One of the major features of the outpouring of the Holy Spirit at Pentecost was the release of revelation through dreams, as quoted by Peter from Joel 2:28. It would seem that the filling of the Holy Spirit awakens the spiritual receiver within us and releases dreams as a normal means of revelation.

Historically, dreams have been a way through which God has spoken to men and women, and the impact of this form of revelation is recorded throughout the Scriptures in both the Old and New Testaments. Furthermore, there is evidence that dreams remain a powerful means of communication used by God today. Through dreams he continues to speak, encourage, inspire and give insight and warning.

The first recorded dream in Scripture was given to Abraham (see Genesis 15:12ff). The narrative records that at sunset Abraham fell into a deep sleep, during which he was conscious of a thick and dreadful darkness. At that point he heard the voice of God. The dream was very detailed, prophesying the future of the chosen people. Abraham heard the Lord promise them land stretching from Egypt in the south to the River Euphrates in the north, but he also discovered that they would first spend 400 years being ill-treated in captivity. Abraham was told in the dream that it would be the fourth generation who would receive the Promised Land.

I have found that in such dreams there is an experience of the awe and fear of God, even though he is unseen. It is like finding yourself in a void, until suddenly you hear the voice of God. This voice can speak a phrase or sentence, as in Abraham's dream, or it can speak a verse from

Scripture. At times in a dream I have heard a voice give me the chapter and verse from a particular biblical book. On waking, I find that the passage completely highlights a situation I am concerned about and confirms God's involvement in it alongside me.

Dreams as inner healing

The Lord often uses dreams as part of an inner healing process whereby unresolved traumas can be released unconsciously. This process is a little like tying our difficult emotions to a balloon, and then releasing that balloon to float freely away.

I met a young man who told me that, after a family row when he was 14, his father told him that he was not their child, but had been adopted. This traumatic news cut deeply into the boy's emotions and haunted him for years. He eventually found healing through two components. The first was prayer, when the power of the cross of Jesus was put between him and those hurtful words spoken by his father. This cut him free from the painful emotions attached to the trauma. The second part of his healing came through a series of dreams in which the effects and images associated with the trauma were released from that part of his mind not normally accessible in everyday waking life.

Dreams to bring a person to Christ

God can use dreams to bring a person to faith in Jesus. In 2001, one of the great successes on the Lions' rugby tour to Australia was the winger Jason Robinson. He started his career playing rugby league for Wigan, where he became a superstar and was chosen to play for Great Britain. Before changing codes to rugby union and joining Sale Rugby Club, he spent a season in Australia playing league. Here he became very rich, which helped to fuel a long-standing drink problem, and although he was very successful he began to feel a great void in his life.

Jason's life changed when he met Inga Iuigamala, who had been a gifted All Black wing before turning to rugby league. The Samoan was also a born-again Christian, and initially Jason found him difficult to understand: he did not drink, go clubbing or tell dirty jokes, but he always seemed so happy. Jason was invited to Inga's home, where he discovered a truly loving and happy family. He decided that he wanted something of what Inga had.

One day after training, Inga took Jason aside and told him that he had had a dream about him the previous night. In the dream Jason stood on the top of the world, and the world was spinning beneath his feet. Then, slowly, it began to crumble. This dream touched Jason incredibly, and he gave his life to Christ. Jason has said that from that day he has not been inside a pub, and his faith in Jesus has given him what booze, cars and girls never could. It has given him peace of mind.

Over a number of years I travelled extensively in India, ministering in the churches of both the north and the south. For many of the people from the Hindu communities who became Christians, one of the characteristics of their conversion was that Jesus had appeared to them in a dream. For some, physical healing and freedom from the torment of demonic spirits was also ministered through dreams. It was often after such a dream that the person would seek a deeper explanation from the Christian community and discover Christ.

Demonically inspired dreams

It is not uncommon for people to experience demonically inspired dreams. These could even be called demonic attacks, because they create fear. The apostle Paul reminded the Christians in Ephesus that now they were followers of Jesus, they were engaged in a battle. This conflict was not against other people, but rather against 'spiritual forces of evil in the heavenly realms' (Ephesians 6:12).

I have had many such experiences in dreams. Once I dreamed that I was walking down a road when I passed a person. As I turned to look at him, I saw a grotesque demonic figure which tried to attack me. I was very startled and fearful, but immediately called upon the name of Jesus. At that point the figure became unable to hurt me, and I woke shaken but safe.

Such demonically inspired dreams are often referred to as 'nightmares'. The Old English word *mare* was a term used for an evil spirit. German, Old Norse, Polish and French have a similar word referring to an evil spirit and associated with such dreams.

Within a pagan culture, dreams can be used as a vehicle for satanic revelation. Through the prophet Isaiah the Lord addresses a group of people in Israel who were seeking revelation in this way. He refers to them as 'a people who continually provoke me to my very face, offering sacrifices in gardens and burning incense on altars of brick; who sit among the graves and spend their nights keeping secret vigil' (Isaiah 65:3–4). The technical term for sitting among the graves and keeping vigil is 'incubation', and in paganism it was believed that by spending a night in a cemetery, the sleeper would be visited by the departed spirit and information or guidance would be imparted. This is why some mediums, spiritists and occult practitioners are often quite right in the revelations they give, but such revelation cannot lead to life. These are deceiving spirits, and often the recipient is bound by an abnormal and terrifying fear after the medium shares the dream with them.

How dreams are received

Significant dreams are received in a number of different ways. On waking, the exact content of the dream is sometimes remembered in vivid detail, and in such dreams everything is significant. When the Lord gave the Babylonian king Nebuchadnezzar a significant dream (see Daniel 2), it was so vivid and troubling that he subsequently had difficulty sleeping. He commanded his puzzled group of astrologers, magicians and enchanters to tell him both the content of his dream and its interpretation; inability to do so would result in their death.

Nebuchadnezzar's abnormal reaction shows something of the awe which a God-inspired dream creates. Daniel, a prophet in his employment, believed that God could give him the revelation and, with his friends, pleaded with God to show him what the dream meant. The Bible records that 'during the night the mystery was revealed to Daniel in a vision' (Daniel 2:19), and the chapter goes on to describe the dream and interpretation in detail. Every detail featured in the dream proved to be significant.

Dreams can also come in fragments, like a jigsaw puzzle. Initially, each part of the dream may seem unrelated, but once all the parts have been written down and meditated upon, the message makes sense and can be understood as the parts are joined together.

Recall

On some occasions, we may have no recollection of having
dreamed during the night at all, but perhaps later in the
day a situation arises which seems familiar to us, and this
triggers a 'dream recall'. The French have the expression
déjà vu, which means literally 'already seen'. It is used to
describe the experience of perceiving a new situation as if
it had occurred before. There are several explanations for
this peculiar feeling, but it is possible that the recall of our
dreams could be one cause. When a dream recall occurs,
you not only see a situation but also have an explanation
for it.

In my book *Riding the Storm*, I recounted a meeting Mary
and I had with the Kansas City Prophets at Holy Trinity
Brompton during a John Wimber conference. Mary and I
were invited with some other leaders to a private meeting
with the prophets, to be held in the church crypt. As we
entered the room and sat down, Bob Jones, who seemed to
be the leader, greeted me with enthusiasm and said how
good it was to see me again. We had never met, and I told
him so. He took some convincing, but it was the truth.
Suddenly he said with relief, 'I've got it,' and went on to
tell me that he had been seeing me in his dreams for the
last two nights. He was having a dream recall. He spoke in
some detail of my past, mentioning disappointments and
times of sadness. He described my Christian ministry and
told me of the ways he 'saw' God developing this. I was
overwhelmed. Then he ended with the words, 'The days
are coming when the Lord will take from you everything
you have built up and relied upon.' This proved only too
true, as I recount in *Riding the Storm*.

Warning dreams

Dreams fall into a number of definable categories, including guidance, encouragement and healing. At times God uses dreams to give an insight into a problem or situation. For example, Eliphaz, one of Job's counsellors, receives the answer to a question he has been asked by Job through a dream, and at the end of a series of dreams he hears the voice of God (see Job 4:12ff).

Particular dreams also come to warn individuals. Elihu, the youngest of Job's counsellors, says they come so that God 'may speak in their ears and terrify them with warnings, to turn man from wrongdoing and keep him from pride, to preserve his soul from the pit, his life from perishing by the sword' (Job 33:16–18). Warning dreams are described throughout the Bible and continue to this day.

For Jacob

Jacob was told in a dream to flee with his two wives from his father-in-law Laban and to return to Canaan. Laban heard about this and pursued him, no doubt intending to retrieve his daughters and the livestock. While he was on the way, however, the Lord appeared to Laban in a dream and warned him not to touch Jacob. As he slept, the Lord said, 'Be careful not to say anything to Jacob, either good or bad' (Genesis 31:24).

At Jesus' birth

There were many warning dreams given to those closely associated with the birth of Jesus. Joseph, Mary's husband, was directed very clearly through warning dreams. Just before Herod's edict commanding the killing of all the children in Bethlehem under the age of two, Joseph had a warning dream. In his dream an angel of the Lord appeared and told him to take Mary and Jesus to Egypt, because Herod intended to search for Jesus and kill him. After Herod's death the angel again appeared to Joseph in a dream and told him to return with his family to Israel. On their return, however, Joseph discovered that Herod had been replaced by his son Archelaus. This made Joseph afraid to return to Judea, and while he was contemplating the situation his apprehension was confirmed by another warning dream, so he travelled north with his family and settled in Nazareth, in the district of Galilee (see Matthew 2).

After Jesus was born, the Magi, or wise men, had travelled from a country in the east to Jerusalem, seeking a king. In their own country they had received a revelation from God to the effect that the king they sought would be found under a star which had recently appeared in the sky. Their subsequent appearance in Jerusalem greatly disturbed Herod, and he arranged a secret meeting with them. He sent them on to Bethlehem, where the Jews believed the Messiah would be born. He instructed the Magi to return to him once they had found the child so that he could go and worship him also. After they had seen Jesus, however, the Magi had a warning dream that led them to return by another route (see Matthew 2:12).

For a non-believer

It is not only those who are followers or seekers of the Lord who have warning dreams. Abimelech was the pagan king of Gerar. When Abraham was travelling in the Negev, he stayed in the city of Gerar and, because he was fearful of the consequences, he falsely let it be known that his wife Sarah was actually his sister. Abimelech heard this and, since he found Sarah attractive, took her into his harem. One night the Lord came to him in a dream, telling him that Sarah was married and warning him that if he slept with her he would be committing adultery. Abimelech pleaded his innocence. He was then instructed to return Sarah to her husband and to ask Abraham to pray for him. If he followed this instruction he would live, but if not, he would die (see Genesis 20).

At Jesus' crucifixion

When Jesus is brought before Pilate, the governor asks him directly whether or not he is the king of the Jews. Jesus affirms that he is. While Pilate is in the middle of dealing with this politically tricky situation, a slave arrives with a message from his wife. She has just had a dream in which she sees that Jesus is innocent, and she advises her husband to have nothing to do with him (see Matthew 27:19).

Today

At a conference where I was speaking on hearing the voice of God, my talks included some material about dreams. At the end of one session I invited questions or contributions from the delegates, and a lady told us of a dream her husband had had while they were on holiday. This had happened abroad some twelve years previously. Her husband had been very disturbed when he woke up, and said that in a dream the Lord had given him a warning about their planned afternoon sightseeing tour. He described the dream in detail, and his wife immediately suggested that they cancel the tour. Her husband was not so sure. He argued that the Lord had shown him the danger in order that he could pray about it and trust the Lord for his protection in the situation. His wife strongly disagreed. She thought the Lord had given him the dream as a warning not to go on the tour. Eventually they went, and during the afternoon the lady's husband was tragically killed in an accident.

From the above examples, it is clear that all such warning dreams given to the emerging prophet must be taken seriously. The kind of warning dreams described above, concerning individuals, are usually fairly simple and self-explanatory. Other warning dreams can be less straightforward to grasp.

Warning dreams for a nation

There are also warning dreams that relate to whole nations. During Joseph's time in Egypt, Pharaoh shared with him two consecutive dreams he had on one particular night (see Genesis 41). In the first dream he was standing on the banks of the River Nile when seven sleek, fat cows appeared, grazing among the reeds. Suddenly another seven cows stood alongside them, but these were skinny and ill fed. As Pharaoh watched, they ate up the fat cows. Such things happen in dreams! Pharaoh woke, and then returned to sleep. His second dream was similar, but this time it involved seven healthy ears of corn growing on a single stem. Seven others appeared, but these had been scorched by a hot east wind. The scorched corn swallowed the healthy corn.

These were not simple dreams. They were highly symbolic, and required an interpretation. As Joseph told his fellow prisoners, Pharaoh's chief cupbearer and baker, 'Do not interpretations [of dreams] belong to God?' (Genesis 40:8)

Repeated dreams

Pharaoh had two very similar dreams with the same message. If this happens, or if a dream is repeated, then, as Joseph said to Pharaoh, 'The reason . . . is that the matter has been firmly decided by God, and God will do it soon' (Genesis 41:32).

I was preaching one morning at our church on the subject of the healing ministry of Jesus. Sitting in the front row were two women from South America, one of whom spoke English and the other only her native language. The English speaker was translating for her friend, but after a while her friend fell asleep – which did not reflect too well on the quality of the preaching, I thought! As she slept, she dreamed, and in her dream she saw an enormous bowl suspended above the congregation. The bowl was filled with oil that was running over the rim and falling on the congregation. Waking up, she shared what she had seen with her friend, and shortly afterwards went back to sleep – whereupon she had an identical dream. The fact that she had the same dream twice led me to believe that God had firmly decided that our church would be a place of healing.

Interpreting dreams

The interpretation of dreams happens in a number of ways. Often the dreamer knows on waking what the dream means, because he or she can interpret the significance of the people or places in the dream. People's characteristics often symbolize a quality, such as faithfulness. Seeing them in a dream conveys a message about the quality rather than the people themselves. This is often the key to the meaning of the dream.

The interpretation of dreams is like the gift of interpreting tongues. Once the dream is told, the interpreter speaks the meaning immediately. It seems to come directly from the lips rather than being processed through the mind. Having listened to Pharaoh recount his dreams, Joseph immediately said, 'The dreams of Pharaoh are one and the same. God has revealed to Pharaoh what he is about to do'

(Genesis 41:25). The interpretation was that there would be seven years of plenty followed by seven years of famine. The dreams were given in order that Pharaoh could take action to store food in the good years, thus preventing severe deprivation in the lean years that would follow.

A little earlier in the story, while he was in prison, Joseph heard the dreams of two men. The first involved Pharaoh's cupbearer. In a dream he saw a vine with three branches. These budded, blossomed and then ripened. In his hand he held Pharaoh's cup. Taking the grapes, he squeezed them and then placed the cup in Pharaoh's hand. It was a picture of restoration. The cupbearer was again in relationship with Pharaoh, handing him wine as he had done before. Joseph told the cupbearer that the three branches symbolized three days. After that period of time he would return to his previous job.

The palace baker then recounted his dream, hoping that it would have a similar interpretation. He dreamed he was carrying three baskets of bread on his head. In the top basket were special breads he had baked for Pharaoh. Suddenly birds came and started to eat this bread. This symbolized something being taken away violently. Joseph told him that the three baskets symbolized three days. The ending, however, was traumatic: 'Within three days Pharaoh will lift off your head and hang you on a tree. And the birds will eat away your flesh' (Genesis 40:19). Joseph had never been one to hold back!

Dreams essentially operate through pictures, symbols and events that vividly impress themselves upon the dreamer. The gift of interpretation can be developed as one grows in spiritual maturity, but others have a strong anointing for this form of revelation and see the meaning easily and quickly. Joseph and Daniel are good examples of people with a strong anointing in this form of revelation.

The appearance of God in a dream

God himself may appear to a person in a dream, although we are not told what form he takes. Jacob had such a visitation when in a dream he saw a ladder that stretched from earth to heaven. As he watched, angels were ascending and descending. At the top of the ladder he saw the Lord, who spoke with him and revealed his nature and his call upon his life (see Genesis 28:12ff). This was a memorable moment for Jacob and was a catalyst for the start of his journey of faith in the living God. God had made an entry into his life.

The Lord also appeared in a dream to Solomon, who was on the verge of his kingly reign. God spoke and invited Solomon to ask of him whatever he would like to be given. The young king replied that he would like a discerning heart that would enable him to govern his people justly (see 1 Kings 3:9). Although Solomon was aware that this dialogue took place in a dream, he also recognized that the promise of God through this means was authentic. That promise was, of course, subsequently fulfilled.

The call of God in a dream

Through dreams God can also reveal his calling and purposes to a person. Joseph was the youngest and favourite son of Jacob and Rachel. He was 17 years old when he had two significant dreams. In the first he was harvesting with his brothers. The sheaf that he bound stood upright and those of his brothers gathered round it and bowed down in homage. This was followed by a similar dream, where 'the sun and moon and eleven stars were bowing down to me' (Genesis 37:9). Joseph saw from this that there would be a time when he would have pre-eminence over both his parents and his brothers. Most unwisely, however, he shared this with them – although the revelation must later have helped him make sense of a very difficult period in his life. God worked deeply in his life to enable him to wear his mantle of authority with integrity.

Wisdom for interpreting dreams

Sharing the interpretation of a dream requires wisdom. Dreams can sometimes be given to lead us to pray and intercede for people and situations, but before sharing details that could cause anxiety or fear, it is advisable to consult mature Christians who have experience in matters of revelation.

Jacob was also a dreamer of the Lord's dreams, and he had learned how to respond. He listened to his son Joseph and then made no comment. It is recorded that '[Joseph's] father kept the matter in mind' (Genesis 37:11). This humble spirit was reflected centuries later in Mary, Jesus' mother, when the shepherds of Bethlehem gave her a revelation concerning the baby. 'Mary treasured up all these things and pondered them in her heart' (Luke 2:19). Often these things must be prayed about, meditated upon and pondered in our hearts before we take any action.

Any form of revelation has the innate ability to create pride, and it is therefore important that we adopt a humble spirit concerning the things we see and hear from God. The apostle Paul told the Christians in Corinth how revelation is inclined to create pride in the heart. He believed that the 'thorn in the flesh' which he experienced was admitted by the Lord to stop him becoming conceited because of what God was showing him in the Spirit (see 2 Corinthians 12:7).

Acting on significant dreams

It has been my experience that dreams often come in batches. Leading up to a New Wine family conference which I was co-hosting with David Pytches, I had a series of five dreams. These came on five consecutive nights and all reflected aspects of God's view of the church in England. Between such batches there usually comes a regular flow of single dreams.

It is important to write down and record all such dreams. Daniel did exactly that: 'Daniel had a dream, and visions passed through his mind as he was lying on his bed. He wrote down the substance of his dream' (Daniel 7:1).

It is helpful to put at the top of the page the date and the place where the dream occurred. Next write out in full the content of the dream as you remember it. Finally, write out your interpretation or the interpretation given by a person with the gifting.

If you do not feel the dream is specifically meant for yourself, it is vital that you discover for whom the dream is meant. If you sense that the dream relates to your church, then you need to give a copy of what you have written down to your church leader. Once this has been passed over, your responsibility ceases and it is then up to the pastor to decide how it is to be communicated further and acted upon.

A person may appear in your dream unconnected to anything else. You may just see his or her face. This may well be the Lord's way of asking you to pray for that person.

Alternatively, in your dream a person may appear in a given situation. Once I saw in a dream a woman I knew slightly; she was pregnant and very frightened of having the baby. I visited her home, and the situation was just as I had seen it in the dream. It is not necessary to mention your dream to the person, and in this case, just as I was preparing to leave after a cup of tea, I simply asked whether the mother-to-be had any apprehensions concerning the birth. She wept and said that she was terrified. I was able to pray for her, and Jesus broke the power of the fear.

If your dream is about the national church or the nation, it is usually given in order that intercession can be made for the area or matter that has been revealed to you. If you are a preacher or teacher, then the Lord may well want you to speak the message in the areas where you have authority.

Dreams can be a precious gift from God and, used wisely, they are undeniably a strategic resource in the prophetic, healing and intercessory ministries of the church.

4

Speaking into People's Lives

> For I did not speak of my own accord, but the Father who
> sent me commanded me what to say and how to say it.
> (John 12:49)

There will be many occasions when the Lord will give the
emerging prophet a word for an individual. The person
concerned may be a complete stranger to the prophet, or
someone quite familiar. Whatever the situation, it is important that we speak out what we have been given by the
Lord, as the word could potentially transform that person
or protect him or her from imminent danger.

Hearing God's word and speaking it to others will be a
major feature of the next significant move of the Spirit. I
believe that this will lead to a period of significant church
growth. In introducing this subject, I would like to recount
two stories – one from Scripture and the other from my
own experience. We shall then consider how these particular prophets received the words from God.

Samuel, Saul and the donkeys of Kish

My scriptural illustration covers a period of four days and

revolves around the story of Samuel and Saul as recorded in 1 Samuel 9–10. Kish, a wealthy landowner, discovers that his donkeys have gone missing. To him this is the equivalent of losing the farm tractors and the family cars at the same time, so he sends his son Saul out with a servant to look for the donkeys. They spend the day tracking through the desert without any success.

At the same time, the prophet Samuel hears God speak to him about an event that is going to happen on the following day. The revelation is very specific and the word concerns an unknown person. This person will appear in town the next morning and will be travelling from the land of Benjamin. Samuel is instructed to anoint him as a national leader, as this person is going to bring about the nation's freedom from Philistine domination. Samuel immediately takes action to get ready for his unknown guest by asking the cook to prepare a special meal for him.

By the second day, Saul and his servant have travelled many miles in search of the donkeys. Eventually they arrive at a city called Zuph. By this time they are very keen to return home. Saul's servant, however, tells him that in Zuph is a man of God who accurately foretells future events. He suggests that they go and consult with him concerning the whereabouts of the donkeys.

As the two men approach the town, they meet girls going to draw water from the well and make enquiries concerning the prophet. They are told that he has just arrived in the town to lead a special religious celebration.

When Saul enters the town, Samuel catches sight of him and, as he looks at him, the Lord says simply, 'This is the man I spoke to you about; he will govern my people' (9:17).

Saul approaches Samuel and asks the way to the prophet's house. Samuel introduces himself, and tells Saul that they will worship together and then share a meal. The following day he will tell Saul all that he has been thinking about. As an aside, he announces that the donkeys have been found, and that Saul is to be the leader for whom the nation has been waiting.

It is at this point that the prophetic word starts to come to Saul. Initially it reveals his lack of confidence and self-worth, and he responds to Samuel by saying that he is from the smallest tribe in Israel and from the most insignificant clan. This is not altogether the truth. The tribe of Benjamin, although reckoned to be the smallest in numbers, was renowned to be full of brave fighters.

Next Samuel takes Saul for a meal. This again is full of prophetic significance. The prophet ordered the food the day before in faith, believing that the unknown leader would come to the town, and he says to the cook, 'Bring the piece of meat I gave you, the one I told you to lay aside' (9:23).

Early in the morning on the following day, Samuel and Saul walk together to the edge of town. During the night Samuel has received more revelation concerning Saul, and he tells his guest to send his servant on while he relays to Saul 'a message from God' (9:27).

Having anointed him with oil in the Lord's name, Samuel proceeds to give Saul 21 prophetic signs to authenticate the word he has spoken over him concerning his call to the leadership of the nation. This is the most detailed revelation to an individual in the Bible.

Samuel refers prophetically to three major meetings which Saul will have as he returns home. First, when he reaches Rachel's tomb, he will meet two men who will inform him that his father's donkeys have been found, and that his father is now worrying about his own safe return (see 10:2).

Second, when he comes to a local landmark known as the 'tree of Tabor', he will meet three men. They will be on their way to worship the Lord at Bethel, one carrying three goats, another three loaves of bread and another a skin of wine. They will greet him and offer him two loaves of bread, which he should accept (see 10:3–4).

Finally, he is to go to Gibeah of God, where there is a Philistine outpost. As he approaches the city he will meet a procession of prophets returning from a celebration. Before them will be an instrumental worship band and the prophets will be prophesying. As this unfolds before him, the Spirit of the Lord will fall powerfully upon him and he will prophesy and undergo a radical inward change (see 10:5–6).

Samuel then answers a question which Saul is obviously thinking but not vocalizing. It concerns what he should do once these things have happened to him. Samuel says, 'Once these signs are fulfilled, do whatever your hand finds to do, for God is with you' (10:7).

When Saul leaves Samuel, all the 21 signs are fulfilled. Eventually Saul meets the procession of prophets and the Spirit comes upon him in power, whereupon he prophesies. Then he continues on his way home.

This is a key example of ministering the prophetic word to an individual. Samuel heard the voice of God clearly and used this information to minister in a very unique and personal way to young Saul. The signs given were a powerful affirmation of the initial word, confirming the fact that he would be the nation's new leader. This word inspired and enabled Saul to understand the present and to have hope for the future.

A word for me in India

The illustration I would like to share from my own experience occurred when I was invited to take a team to India and lead a number of conferences. It had been envisaged that we would also go to Sri Lanka in response to an invitation from Bishop Swithian. Just before we left the UK, I had a call from the bishop to say that because of the deteriorating political situation it would not be safe for a team to visit Sri Lanka, especially as we had planned to minister in the north of the island. He asked, however, whether I might go out there on my own and speak at a number of smaller meetings which he would organize. This was not our normal practice, but under the circumstances it seemed to be the right course of action.

The plan was that I should go by myself to Sri Lanka first, and then meet our team in Madras, where our initial conference was to be held. I duly visited the island, and then flew up to Madras. As I left the aircraft and headed towards immigration, I could see our team standing with the local bishop, waiting to greet me. I handed over my New Zealand passport and the official thumbed through the pages. He wanted to know where my visa for India was. I told him that this was my fifth visit and I had never needed a visa previously. Unbeknown to me, however, the situation had changed and I now needed a visa. The official said that he had no alternative but to send me back to Sri Lanka.

Arriving back on the island, I was perplexed and bewildered. The following morning I went down to the Indian High Commission to see if I could get the necessary visa. After a three-hour wait in temperatures that soared to over 100 degrees Fahrenheit, my request was refused. The clerk told me that the only way I could obtain the visa was to return to my country of origin.

For the next three days I rejoined the queue, hoping to find a clerk who might allow the impossible. If I was refused on the third day, I decided, I would fly back to the UK. On that final morning, however, I managed to see a senior officer who – amazingly – was willing to make an exception.

The next morning I flew to Trivandrum, which is the major city in the southern state of Kerala. That was where our team had planned to minister after Madras. I had arrived a day early, and was rather dejected. Having found a place to stay, I wandered down to the area where the woodcarvers work.

After a while, still full of self-pity, I started to meander back. Then suddenly, to my surprise, I saw a white man pass by carrying a cross. He and I were probably the only white faces in the whole of the city. I walked on alone for some time, but then felt a strong inner conviction that I should meet this man. Retracing my footsteps, I started to run down the road in the direction I had last seen him walking.

Eventually I caught up with him. It was Arthur Blessitt, the American evangelist. I had met him once at a conference in the UK, but he obviously did not remember me. When I approached him, he just kept walking as if I was invisible. Suddenly he stopped and leaned his cross against the railings of a fence. Then he told me the following story.

At the break of day he had left Cape Comorin, the southernmost tip of India, to walk the 600 miles to Goa. When a European walks through an Indian village, nearly everyone comes to watch. That morning was no exception and, through his translator, Arthur had spoken to thousands of people by lunchtime. After lunch, however, it was as if he had been made invisible. Hardly anyone noticed his presence. As he walked on, he heard the Lord say to him that he wanted him to be in Trivandrum by five o'clock. He looked at his map and calculated that if he just kept walking for three hours, he would be able to do it.

Later in the afternoon, he asked the Lord again. This time the Lord said to him that he wanted him in Trivandrum by five o'clock to meet a man. As Arthur told me this, the alarm on his digital watch sounded five bleeps. Looking straight at me, he said, 'You are the man.' At that moment the Holy Spirit came powerfully upon us both.

Arthur laid his hands on my head and started to prophesy. He said that although I did not understand my situation and what had happened to me, I was nevertheless right in the will and plans of God. If the Lord opens a door, he said, no one can shut it and, conversely, if he shuts a door, no one can open it. Finally, he said that the most important aspect of my relationship with my heavenly Father is not *what I do* for him but rather *who I am* with him. Over many years I have returned to these words for encouragement and comfort.

These examples of biblical and contemporary prophets hearing the voice of God show just how life-changing this ministry can be. It is vital for the emerging prophet to hear God's voice and to know how to recognize his word. The prophet needs to be consistently waiting on God to see and hear him.

Characteristics of an eagle

The prophet's ministry of seeing and hearing the word of God is often likened to the actions of an eagle, which is a symbol of the prophetic. This is why many old churches have their church Bible resting on a lectern shaped like the wings of an eagle.

I once telephoned the ornithological department of London Zoo and asked to speak to the person responsible for the care of the eagles. He told me about many of the eagle's characteristics, which I discovered are also observable in the emerging prophet.

For instance, the eagle does not fly, as most birds do, by flapping its wings, but instead waits for the air currents. As the eagle catches a current, it expands its wings and simply rides on the thermals to great heights. The Lord says through Isaiah that those who wait on him will 'soar on wings like eagles' (Isaiah 40:31).

As the eagle hovers, its entire body moves except its head, which holds its position. From that hovering position the eagle has both a panoramic and a magnified view, and its eyesight is three times more accurate than that of a human. In ancient Israel the prophets were called 'seers' because they were able to see the things that only the Spirit of God saw. They saw a clear, magnified view through revelation as they waited on the Lord and were caught up by his Spirit.

Hearing the voice of God

Revelations are thoughts, ideas or perceptions given by the Holy Spirit which can be both seen and heard. A revelation can be received through the audible voice of God. There are two such audible voices, the internal and the external. The external voice, which is unusual, is God speaking to you in your own language. When the Lord called Samuel as a young boy, Samuel thought it was the human voice of Eli the priest (see 1 Samuel 3). God used the Hebrew language and spoke in a normal voice.

How many people hear such a voice? I have often spoken on this subject in conferences where there have been up to 350 delegates. During the talk I have asked for a show of hands from people who have heard the external, audible voice of God. Perhaps twelve people will indicate that they have. I then ask if they have heard such a voice more than once. Only one or two will acknowledge that this has happened.

The internal, audible voice

Normally when God speaks to us, it is through an internal, audible voice. The word may come as an impression or as a phrase or sentence which passes through the heart. There is a recurring phrase in the Old Testament which introduces a revelation from God. The prophet will say, 'The word of the Lord came . . .' In Hebrew this literally means 'a whispering'. Elijah experienced this in a cave on Mount Horeb after he had fled the persecution of Jezebel (see 1 Kings 19:12). At the cave entrance he encountered a powerful wind, an earthquake and fire, but the Lord was not communicating through these – he spoke through a 'still small voice', or a 'gentle whisper' as the NIV translates it.

When I receive such words, they often come like a small pebble being dropped into a pond. Once the pebble breaks the surface, waves radiate out from it. A young woman we know was talking with me, sharing how she had for some time suffered from continuous stomach pains. Her doctor had conducted a thorough examination and, although he could not diagnose any particular physical problem, he had put her on a course of medication. As she was sharing this with me, the word 'anxiety' fell into my heart. This was like the pebble dropping into the water. Immediately I asked her what she was anxious about. She was then able to share an ongoing problem in her life. The word had come in order that the Lord might heal her.

It would seem in the illustration of Samuel and Saul that the prophet may well have heard both these audible voices.

> Now the day before Saul came, the Lord had revealed this to Samuel: 'About this time tomorrow I will send you a man from the land of Benjamin. Anoint him leader over my people Israel; he will deliver my people from the hand of the Philistines. I have looked upon my people, for their cry has reached me.' (1 Samuel 9:15–16)

Such words could simply have been the inner, audible voice of God, but they were followed by what could have been the external, audible voice. When Samuel caught sight of Saul, the Lord said to him very clearly, 'This is the man I spoke to you about' (9:17). This would have been what Arthur Blessitt also heard from God when he said to me, 'You are the man.'

The word through vision

There are also revelations from God that are received through visions. In Genesis 15:1 it is recorded that 'the word of the Lord came to Abram in a vision: "Do not be afraid, Abram. I am your shield, your very great reward."'

Visions can be used powerfully to minister to individuals. On one occasion a Norwegian pastor asked me to pray for him. As I prayed, I saw a number of snow-capped mountains appearing above the skyline. Then the sun rose and started to melt the peaks. I thought that what I saw was a picture of his congregation, and that there were areas of extreme coldness which the Lord was starting to melt. As I shared what I had seen, however, there seemed to have been a misunderstanding, because the pastor abruptly walked out of the meeting room and left the house.

The following Sunday he came to our church, and at the end of the evening he approached me in tears. He described what had happened to him since we had last met. When I had spoken to him, he had thought I was saying that he had a heart of ice, and it had made him very angry. The following day he went to Westminster Cathedral and sat by himself in a chapel. When he looked up, to his amazement he saw above him – in three dimensions – Jesus nailed to a cross. As he watched, the vision became increasingly clear. He found himself weeping silently as he realized what a cold-hearted person he really was. After a time the vision faded. This had a profound and life-changing effect on him. What was interesting for me was that I had interpreted the vision differently (I had applied the coldness to the congregation generally), but God used it to speak personally to the pastor.

There will be times in a public meeting when the prophet will have an internal vision and will hear the internal, audible voice, and the message will relate to someone in the gathering. I was leading a meeting at our church one day when suddenly I saw a large pine forest in a vision. As I looked, I knew it was somewhere in Canada. In the depths of the forest I saw a majestic waterfall and sitting on a rock beside it was a young man who was grieving as a result of a broken relationship.

At the appropriate time in the service, I shared what I was seeing and invited the person to come up for prayer. The young man who responded was called Steve. He was a New Zealander who had been living in Canada, where he had met and fallen in love with a young woman. She had called off the relationship and he had gone to seek solace in the forest. The situation I had described in the vision was exactly as he had experienced it. Again this was to be a life-changing experience for Steve.

The river of revelation

I have come to see that receiving revelation for others is like standing on the bank of a river. The revelation comes to us flowing from the future, through the present, and into the past. If you look upstream, you are looking into the future and seeing what is to come. If you look straight ahead, you are seeing the present. If you look downstream, you are seeing the past and are viewing what has already happened. As we consider Jesus and the prophets, it becomes apparent that they received revelation from all these areas.

In John 4, when Jesus encounters a woman near a well in Samaria, he engages her in conversation concerning himself and the Holy Spirit. She indicates that she would like to receive what Jesus has described as 'living water'. He tells her to go and bring her husband, and she replies that she is not married. Jesus looks downstream into what has already taken place in her life and says as a result of revelation, 'You are right when you say you have no husband. The fact is, you have had five husbands.' Jesus then looks across the river into the present and says to the woman, 'The man you now have is not your husband' (4:17–18). Finally, he widens the scope of the conversation and looks upstream, to a time when 'true worshippers will worship the Father in spirit and truth' (v. 23).

On another occasion, Jesus, looking upstream into the future, speaks a prophetic word to Martha: 'Your brother will rise again at the last day.' Similarly, Joseph looked upstream when he spoke words to Pharaoh's cupbearer and baker concerning what was to come for them in just three days.

Noonie, one of our daughters, was returning home by taxi from an office meeting when she realized that the taxi driver was not one of the familiar ones used by her firm. He was of a foreign nationality, and when she asked where he was from he replied that he came from the Ukraine. As she spoke to him she found herself looking downstream into what had passed in his life and saying, 'You're not a taxi driver; you're a doctor.' This made him catch his breath, and when he asked how she knew she replied that Jesus had shown her.

Noonie then went on to say to him that he had been forced to flee from the Ukraine and had to leave behind a girl with waist-length dark hair whose name was Anna. At this the taxi driver started to shake. He said that Anna was the name of his daughter, and he had indeed had to leave her behind. Noonie told him that Jesus wanted him to know that he fully understood his situation and would like to be with him in it. There is nothing like the prophetic word to connect a person to Jesus! Noonie arrived home safely, after the taxi driver had calmed down . . .

At times you will find yourself looking upstream into someone's future. Our son Timothy lives in Harrow on the Hill and on one occasion he and his brother Jonathan were having a drink together at the local pub. A man in his early thirties came in and sat down by himself at a nearby table. He kept watching them and then suddenly stood up and walked over to their table. Looking at Jonathan, he said, 'I see that you are a man of integrity.' Jonathan was taken completely by surprise. 'Have you anything to say to me?' the stranger continued. Jonathan found himself saying, 'Jesus loves you,' and at that point the young man started to weep.

Jonathan suddenly heard the inner, audible voice of God speaking to him. Repeating what he heard, he said simply, 'I see you are dying.' 'Yes,' came the quiet reply, 'I am dying of AIDS.' My sons invited the stranger to join them. He was obviously looking for someone to listen to him and soon told Tim and Jonathan something of what had happened to him. Being diagnosed with AIDS had sent him into a panic and, distraught, he had boarded a train that morning and got off at Harrow. He had spent most of the day walking round the town asking God continuous questions: 'If you are God, how can I possibly know you?', 'What will happen to me when I die?', 'Is there some way that you can communicate with me?'

Finally, completely exhausted, he had walked into the pub. As he scanned the other customers, his eyes fell on Jonathan and he had a growing impression that somehow this man had the answer to his questions. Together, Jonathan and Tim tried as best they could to respond to those questions, and by the end of the evening the man had come to realize that the answer lay with Jesus Christ. They told him of how, in his death and resurrection, Jesus had dealt with the problem of our separation from God and how, in Jesus, a believer could receive forgiveness and eternal life. The man asked for prayer, and they prayed for him together. There, at a pub table, that man received hope.

Seeing the calling on an individual

Emerging prophets will minister God's word to an individual in a variety of ways. Sometimes you will see God's potential in a person and call it into being. Jesus' foremost disciple was Peter, whom, when he was circumcised on the eighth day, his mother named Simon. This has been interpreted as meaning 'like a reed', easily blown in the wind, or 'one who hears God'. Jesus changed this, however. After Simon had confessed his belief in Jesus as the Messiah, Jesus replied, 'You are Peter [meaning "rock"], and on this rock I will build my church' (Matthew 16:18). The prophetic word indicated Simon Peter's potential to be a leader with rock-like qualities, although this was to take time to show itself fully.

On other occasions you will see God's gifting of a person and call it into being. Paul reminded Timothy to fulfil the gifting which the prophets spoke over him: 'Do not neglect your gift, which was given you through a prophetic message when the body of elders laid their hands on you' (1 Timothy 4:14).

A while back I was leading a day conference based at a church in the South Island city of Christchurch, New Zealand. It was late in the afternoon when we had a time of ministry, and it seemed to me that the Lord was anointing many of the delegates with gifts for the fivefold ministries – apostles, prophets, evangelists, pastors and teachers. I invited the various groups to come for prayer.

We were praying particularly for the evangelists when a young man came in and walked to the front of the building to see what was going on. I tried as best as I could to explain what was happening as the power of God fell on the people, but he said that he did not know what his particular gift was. That afternoon, he told me, he had set out to come to the conference, but had got distracted in the park. He had met a group of young people and had spent the time talking to them about Jesus. Just before joining us, he said, he had prayed with a young man who wanted to become a follower of Jesus.

I said to him that he was clearly an evangelist, and asked whether he would like me to pray over him. As I did this in Jesus' name, I called for a full release of this gifting and affirmed him in it. The last time I saw this young man, he was prostrate on the floor of the building. A year later he went to Australia, led many to faith in Jesus and planted a church. The gifting had been confirmed in him through the word, giving him the confidence and direction he needed.

A prophet can bring much encouragement to the ongoing call of God. When our time came to leave Chorleywood, we did not have a new home to go to. The staff at our new church in London had been looking everywhere for a house for us, but to no avail. The problem with having seven children plus husbands, wives and friends was that we needed a five-bedroom home. In London this is almost impossible without mammoth expenditure.

Time went by, and our farewell evening was almost upon us. On a Tuesday morning in late August, Mary and I were leaving early to go and see friends in Hampshire. I was putting a few things in the boot of the car when Graham Cleveland walked past. Graham works in the City of London and leaves Chorleywood before 7 a.m. each morning. He stopped by my car, and said that he had been praying for us that very morning. In his prayers he had been asking the Lord to lead us to a new home. He told us that God had spoken to him, but he had not expected to have the opportunity to speak with us so soon. He was very surprised to find that we were already up and about. He told me that the Lord had said that two weeks from that day, in the morning, we would know where we were going to live in London. I noted the relevant day in my diary.

The Tuesday in question duly arrived. At 10.30 a.m. the telephone rang. It was Kim Ashman from our new church in London. A five-bedroom home had become available just that morning. The family to whom it had been rented had pulled out, and we were invited to have it instead. Mary and I jumped into the car and within two hours we had seen and accepted it.

Affirming the new

Jesus is in the life-changing business. Paul reminded the believers in Corinth, 'If anyone is in Christ, he is a new creation; the old has gone, the new has come!' (2 Corinthians 5:17). Often the Lord will allow the emerging prophet to see something of what his Spirit has been doing in a person, so that the individual can be encouraged and affirmed.

Jesus had never met Nathanael until he was introduced to him by Philip (see John 1:45ff). His first words to him were, 'Here is a true Israelite, in whom there is nothing false' (v. 47). Jesus was looking into the present situation and what he was seeing was incredibly affirming to Nathanael. A 'true Israelite' is someone whose inner life is right in the sight of God. For this to be so, Nathanael must privately and secretly have searched his heart and sought to deal with those things that had separated him from God. Nobody could have known the struggles and heartaches he must have been through.

I was speaking at a European conference and had an excellent translator who appeared to be a very sensitive and mature person. Before one evening meeting we met with others to pray. As I looked at the translator, I started to see that she had experienced a traumatic childhood, characterized by various forms of abuse. Something in particular had happened which had tormented her all her life. That was in the past, but I also saw that, secretly and unknown to anyone else, she had spent much time in prayer sorting out her life with Jesus. This had already led to a deep and real healing. After we had prayed as a group, I told her what I had seen concerning her past life and the new things that were happening in her heart. She started to weep quietly. After I had returned home I received an e-mail from her. She said that all I had spoken was true, and as a result she felt incredibly loved and affirmed by Jesus.

Recognizing characteristics in individuals

My wife Mary often has a joke at my expense. Sometimes when we are out together I see a person I think we know, and I draw Mary's attention to the fact. She looks up and tells me not to be silly – the person looks vaguely the same, but is definitely not the one we know!

For many years I pondered this. Why did I so often see a person I knew superimposed upon a person I did not know? Once I was speaking at a conference for young leaders at Ashburnham Place, and during one talk a young man appeared at the door and stood listening. As soon as I saw him I thought it was my eldest son, Jonathan, which surprised me because at the time he was supposed to be in the USA with David Parker, a Vineyard pastor. I was just about to greet the young man in a fatherly way when I realized that it was not Jonathan at all.

I suddenly understood that the Holy Spirit was trying to reveal something to me. He was showing me that the characteristics of my son were also the characteristics of the young man in the doorway. At the time Jonathan was working on the staff of a local church as a youth pastor. He was also a worship leader and was learning to minister in the prophetic.

Later that day I sought out the young man who had stood listening at the door, and found out that he had come down from London to be alone and seek God concerning his future. After we had spoken for some time, I told him that I thought Jesus was calling him to be a youth pastor as well as to lead worship. I also said that I thought he had a special prophetic anointing on him. These, he replied, were the three things he had been asking Jesus about in prayer.

Since that day, whenever I see one thing and think I am seeing another, I always ask myself this question: What is it about the person I know that the Lord wants me to speak over this person I do not know?

It is also important that those prophesied to should weigh carefully what has been spoken over them. Normally a word spoken to you will fit into the overall pattern of your life. The young man who appeared to be like my son was able to look back and judge what I spoke to him in the context of what God had already been saying over the years. If a word is given which is in any sense directional, however, it is essential that you share this with church leaders before you take any action. This is a cardinal rule concerning directional prophecy.

In addition to weighing carefully what is said, if you believe God is speaking to you through the prophet, then you have to fulfil the prophetic word. This may seem obvious in theory, but it is a matter of utmost importance. Fulfilment will not necessarily happen if you remain passive. Recently I kept being made conscious of a particular young man. Whenever I looked at him, the Spirit seemed to be saying that he was being called to assist in the youth work of the church. Eventually I conveyed this to him. He said that he had sometimes wondered about doing this, but had taken no action. God's plan would only be fulfilled, it appeared, if he *actively* offered himself to work with the youth department.

Highlighting and seeing

Sometimes the prophet is drawn to a person and something about that individual is highlighted. An interesting illustration of this comes in one of the most moving films I have ever seen, *Schindler's List*. This film was shot in black and white, but there is one scene where the Jews are being taken out of the ghetto for extermination and among the crowd is a little girl wearing a light pink coat. She appears in colour for a fraction of a second. A little later in the film, the pink coat is seen briefly amongst a heap of tragic, discarded black and white clothing in a death camp. Many people I know who saw the film never noticed that glimpse of the light pink coat.

Seeing in a prophetic way is rather like learning to recognize another colour. This is how the Lord draws your attention to a person or a situation. When this happens, it will not go away. The emerging prophet will keep being drawn back to it.

I was speaking at a conference for young leaders in Finland. After the first meeting there was a break, and as I went for coffee my attention was drawn to a young woman whom I thought I knew. I kept wondering where we had met. Maybe she had visited our church, or attended a New Wine Conference, or had even come to our home. None of these seemed to fit, however.

I looked at her at least three times and on the last occasion, to my surprise, the Lord said to me, 'She ran away from home.' A little later I introduced myself to her and asked her if, at the age of 14, she had run away from home. She was visibly shaken when I said this and asked me how I knew, saying that only members of her immediate family were aware of it. Jesus had told me, I said. I went away that day wondering what had been the point of such a revelation.

On the final day of the conference the young woman sought me out to tell me that the word had started a powerful transforming work in her heart. She said she had always believed that Jesus was full of love for people, and that he heard and answered prayer, but she had never felt that Jesus loved her in a personal way. Since the word had come to her, all of that had changed. She said that if Jesus could tell a person from another country – someone who did not speak her language or know anything about her – things that only her family knew, then he indeed knew all about her and really did love her.

The prophetic word is enormously powerful when it is used in ministering to an individual, whether it comes through a dream, a vision, or a picture, through recognizing characteristics or highlighting issues, or through hearing the audible voice of God.

5

The Nature of the Prophetic Word

My heart is broken within me;
all my bones tremble.
I am like a drunken man,
like a man overcome by wine,
because of the Lord
and his holy words.
(Jeremiah 23:9)

The Holy Spirit operates in the emerging prophet in a number of ways. Often the prophet will sense a 'bubbling up' of the word. This word seems to have its origin from within and, like the water from a spring, it bubbles up into the conscious mind. There are also seasons, however, when the Holy Spirit comes upon the prophet so powerfully that he or she is hardly able to stand under the weight. In this case, people who are normally rational and in control may find themselves stuttering to speak the word, and at times may even bend double and fall to the ground or collapse in a seat after speaking.

One summer I was invited to speak at the Focus conference organized by Holy Trinity Brompton. Two of the leaders, Nicky and Sila Lee, asked me to pray for them. As I prayed, I felt a surge of pins and needles all over my body, a sensation that continued as I spoke. I have found that this is not uncommon in such circumstances, and sometimes it has led me to say to those for whom I am praying, 'I think I'm speaking prophetically over you.'

As I prayed for Nicky and Sila, my arms started to make a circular movement and I found myself saying that what God was calling them to do would get larger and larger. Little did any of us know that in the next few years they would write a book together on marriage (*The Marriage Book* published by HTB) and its popularity would be such that, through the Alpha network, it would reach all the nations of the world.

Compulsion to speak out the word

The prophetic word impacts the prophet first of all, and brings a divine compulsion to speak out the revelation. This may or may not involve physical manifestations, but the prophet Jeremiah, dealing with this aspect of the prophetic word, says,

> So the word of the Lord has brought me
> insult and reproach all day long.
> But if I say, 'I will not mention him
> or speak any more in his name,'
> his word is in my heart like a fire,
> a fire shut up in my bones.
> I am weary of holding it in;
> indeed, I cannot.
> (Jeremiah 20:8–9)

Later he says, 'My heart is broken within me; all my bones tremble. I am . . . like a man overcome by wine, because of the Lord and his holy words' (23:9).

The prophetic word is charged with energy and power, and it is also effective and creative. It does what God intends it to do. Referring to the prophetic word, the writer to the Hebrews says, 'The word of God is living and active. Sharper than any double-edged sword, it penetrates even to dividing soul and spirit, joints and marrow; it judges the thoughts and attitudes of the heart' (Hebrews 4:12).

The word is living and gives life

The prophetic word is also living, and it has within it the power to create life – as we see at the beginning of time, at the Creation: 'And God said, "Let there be light," and there was light' (Genesis 1:3).

One day I returned home to find Mary sitting with a woman who was in great distress. Her husband had left her and she was going through a period of extreme stress. For a couple of hours we listened to her going over and over her story, and during this time we said nothing, but just listened.

Eventually I drove her home, and as we journeyed she kept talking. We arrived at the place where she was staying and just before she got out of the car, I said my first and only words to her. I had been praying as we travelled and had heard the Lord say, 'I understand.' So I said to her, very simply, 'Jesus understands.' Although it was so simple, this was a prophetic word.

Some time later, she made contact with us again and I was surprised and delighted to hear that she had become a Christian and had joined her local church. Her faith had come alive through hearing the simple words, 'Jesus understands'. In her distress these words had kept repeating themselves in her mind, because the Spirit had given them. Eventually she said to Jesus that if he really did understand, then he had to help her. It was at this point that the healing could begin.

The word does what God sends it to do

The prophetic word is active and is able to do what God sends it to do. Isaiah writes this about the activity of the prophetic word:

> As the rain and the snow
> come down from heaven,
> and do not return to it
> without watering the earth
> and making it bud and flourish,
> so that it yields seed for the sower
> and bread for the eater,
> so is my word that goes out from my mouth:
> It will not return to me empty,
> but will accomplish what I desire
> and achieve the purpose for which I sent it.
> (Isaiah 55:10–11)

Such a word is likened to rain, snow and dew that falls continuously and builds up over time. It may not take effect immediately, but will quietly work towards its fulfilment. In this situation the word is spoken to affirm what God has already said in other ways.

I have a friend who has been very successful in the City of London and is married with a young family. There was an event in the City that we were both attending, and as I journeyed to it, my friend came to mind. I heard the Lord say clearly that he was calling him into full-time ordained Christian ministry.

At the event I finally saw my friend across the room and went over to talk to him. He was laughing with those around him, and I leaned over to him and said lightly, 'Dave, I wouldn't joke too much, because the Lord is calling you to full-time ordained ministry.' He went suddenly quiet and left the room. Later I found him sitting outside on a bench, shaking and crying.

It emerged that for a number of months my friend had been contemplating the idea of offering himself for such a ministry. He knew that financially it would be very costly, and he felt the sacrifice would be too much. That very morning, however, he had prayed that if the Lord were really calling him, he would give him some kind of confirmation. The word spoken did what God intended it to do, but it is still moving towards its fulfilment. Dave is now in the process of preparation for full-time ministry.

The directive word

Where the prophetic word is active, it can also be directive. The Lord sends the word to direct the prophet to certain places and people. Isaiah, for example, is told by the Lord, 'Go out . . . to meet Ahaz at the end of the aqueduct of the Upper Pool, on the road to the Washerman's Field. Say to him, "Be careful, keep calm and don't be afraid. Do not lose heart . . ."' (Isaiah 7:3–4).

In the New Testament, there are many instances of directional prophecy in the Acts of the Apostles. Philip was a young church leader who, because of persecution, left Jerusalem and went down to the northern capital of Samaria. Here he spoke about Jesus and the kingdom of God. The power of God accompanied his speaking, and many people not only believed in Jesus but were healed and set free from demons.

On a Sunday before Christmas one year, I returned home from our church and after lunch sat down to read the

Sunday Times. The front page was all about the many young people who were living and sleeping rough on the streets of London. This was common knowledge, of course, and I turned over to the next page. Here the headline read, 'Michelle cries herself to sleep at night', and the story was accompanied by a photograph of a young girl leaning against a shop window. As I looked at the picture and read about the girl's situation, I started to cry. It was as if I heard the Lord say very emphatically, 'Find her.' I shared with Mary what I sensed God was saying, and she agreed that it was from the Lord.

After the evening service at our church, Mary prepared some flasks of hot coffee and I travelled into London with my friend Arthur. Although I had lived in Chorleywood for 30 years, I did not know London at all well. By nature I am not a city person. London is a big place, and we had no real idea where to go. We parked our car near Trafalgar Square and decided to start by walking up the Strand. There were very few people about, but in many of the doorways we saw cardboard tents or little groups of people huddled together in sleeping bags. As we walked, we prayed together that the Lord would guide us.

At the top of the Strand we crossed over and began to walk back. We were halfway down the road when I saw a group of ten or twelve figures huddled in the porch of a shop. As I looked at them I heard the Holy Spirit say, 'This is the place.' We stopped by the group – young people mostly in their early teens, who had covered themselves with blankets. Arthur asked if any of them would like coffee, and soon everyone was drinking.

I noticed an older man leaning against the shop window. He said his name was Tim, and he was 27 years old. I could tell that he was having trouble breathing and asked him what the problem was. He had been on heroin, he said, and was trying to come off it by using a heroin substitute. His chest had become badly infected. I asked him whether he would like me to pray for him and ask Jesus to heal him. He was rather surprised at the offer, but said that he wouldn't mind if I thought it would help. As I was praying for him in Jesus' name, he suddenly asked what was happening to him. I asked him to describe what he meant. He said the whole of his chest was being filled with heat and he felt his breathing was returning to normal. I explained to him that it was the Spirit of Jesus bringing him healing.

While I was praying for Tim, I was conscious that someone was watching me. Looking up, I recognized the face from the picture in the newspaper, and realized that this was the girl we had come to find.

Then Michelle asked me whether I would talk with her, and she began the conversation by asking me whether I would believe what she was going to tell me. She said that she had told her story to many people, and nobody had believed her. On her sixteenth birthday, she and some friends had gone to a local disco to celebrate. At the end of the evening she and one of these friends had got into a car with two men who had brought them down to London and held them in a flat for a number of weeks. Recently she and her friend had escaped, and they were now living rough on the streets. I asked her why she had not contacted her parents, and she said that she was too frightened. I also asked whether she had told the police, and she indicated that she had, but they had not believed the story. After we had talked, she asked whether I could get in touch with her parents to find out whether they would welcome her home. I wrote the telephone number on my hand and said I would do what I could.

Early the following morning I telephoned the number

and told a bewildered father that I had been talking with his daughter in London. He seemed to be in shock, dropping the phone and calling out to his wife. She was overwhelmed by the news. Six months had lapsed since Michelle's disappearance, and she had almost given up hope of ever seeing her daughter again. She asked whether I would be able to bring Michelle home. That evening I returned to London. I had not arranged a rendezvous with Michelle, but I went back to the place where I had met her the previous night. She was not there.

I simply prayed as I walked around the area. It was late and very cold, and I saw a group of men sitting in the corner of a shop doorway, huddling together to keep each other warm. I offered them some soup. One of them commented that he found comfort from some words in the Bible where Jesus had spoken about his Father's house. As I knew this particular passage off by heart, I delighted him by reciting it. I had just finished this when I looked up and there, standing next to me, out of nowhere, was Michelle.

She asked whether I had been in contact with her parents and I told her that they were thrilled with the news and were looking forward to having her home again. Then she asked if I would drive her back home, and I sensed the Holy Spirit indicating to me that I should take her the following morning. This time we arranged a meeting place, and she said that she would sleep in a particular doorway and I should pick her up from there.

The next morning was Christmas Eve. I arrived once again in London, picked Michelle up and brought her back to our own home, where Mary had cooked a big breakfast. After this we drove together to Michelle's home city in the north. I had thought that I might take the opportunity of the long drive to share with her the way in which Jesus had initiated our meeting, but it was a very cold and frosty morning and the inside of the car was warm, and within minutes she was asleep.

When we arrived on the outskirts of the city, I woke her to ask for directions to her home. Michelle's father had taken the day off work and he was there with her mother to welcome her back. Michelle asked whether I would stay with her at first while she renewed contact with her parents, and so I went in, had coffee, and then suggested that it was time for me to go.

Just as I was getting up to leave, her mother mentioned that Michelle suffered from a skin allergy, and I suggested that she might like me to pray for her. As I prayed in Jesus' name, Michelle asked in a puzzled way what was happening to her. She said that her whole body was full of fire and she was unable to move from her position on the sofa. I took the opportunity then of telling her how God had directed me through his Spirit to London, with the explicit purpose of finding her. I told her that what she was experiencing was the power of God on her life. I also told her that Jesus loved her and suggested that she just welcomed him into her heart and made her peace with God.

Watching and listening, her mother said that she had been so stressed over the last six months and was in a chronic state of health. She also allowed me to pray with her, and a similar thing happened to her as to her daughter. When I finally left, Michelle was sitting on the sofa with her mother, and neither of them was able to move!

The risk of looking foolish

At times the emerging prophet will have thoughts which seem to be directional, but the only way to know whether it is the Spirit of God speaking is to do what you sense God is indicating. There have been times, however, when I have done this and the 'word' has had no particular relevance. Sometimes a person may come to mind and I feel I should go and see them straight away. I make my way to their home, only to find that they are out. Or I sense that I should go somewhere and I see somebody I think I should speak with, but in the context there turns out to be no particular relevance in doing this. As the case of Michelle shows, however, it is important that we do step out in faith whenever we sense that it may be God speaking to us. Surely it is better to take action and run the risk of looking foolish than to do nothing and perhaps let a vital chance slip away.

The revealing word

The prophetic word is able to penetrate to the centre of our being, and is able to distinguish between what comes from us or from the enemy, and what comes from God's Spirit.

At one of our Schools for Prophets, a lady asked me a question regarding the ways in which God speaks. She said that often she would sit down to write and an invisible power would take hold of her hand and she would find herself writing automatically. She found the words she wrote beautiful and inspiring. She had hardly finished speaking, however, when I heard a prophetic word for her. I said simply, 'It's the enemy of Jesus who is doing this.' Immediately she fell to the floor and started to behave in a very strange way. She seemed to be struggling to free herself from something that was attached to her throat. I commanded everything that did not belong to the Spirit of God to leave her in the name of Jesus. There was a climax before she went very still. Then she sat up, asking what had happened. Here the prophetic word was penetrating and revealing.

The healing word

The prophetic word is also able to heal. In the Old Testament the psalmist writes of the time when God sent his word and healed the people (see Psalm 107:20). In the New Testament a centurion comes to Jesus asking him to heal his servant. Jesus says that he will go to his home and grant his request. The centurion replies that he is not worthy to have Jesus visit his home, but asks Jesus just to say the word (see Matthew 8:1ff). He believed that healing would come to his servant through the saying of the word.

The unpredictable word

The prophetic word is powerful and unpredictable. In Psalm 29 David likens it to lightning and thunder. Lightning strikes without notice and comes from the most unlikely directions. David refers to lightning splitting open the cedars of Lebanon (v. 5) and twisting the oaks. These trees symbolize something strong that cannot be split or twisted, yet the lightning – like the word of God – can suddenly and unexpectedly do this.

Mary and I started our ministry in Camborne, Cornwall. After I had finished at theological college a friend and I moved our family's possessions down to Camborne in an old hire van. The next day I returned to London and picked up Mary and our young son Jonathan to make the long journey to Cornwall. The further west we travelled, the darker the sky became, and sheets of rain began to crash onto the windscreen of our Mini. To add to our difficulties, the windscreen wipers packed up. Eventually we arrived at the new house, tired and dejected.

The house was in darkness, and once inside we tripped over packing cases and a jumbled assortment of furniture.

The electricity ran by meter and, of course, we did not have the appropriate coins. I had to go next door and borrow enough money to bring light into the house. We were alone, far from friends, and it was dark and teeming with rain.

Suddenly a knock sounded on the door. Standing there in the rain was a man from London whom we had known for many years. He smiled, but did not speak, and walked with me into the kitchen where we had a little Formica table. He then took five small loaves from a paper bag and placed them on the table, followed by two small fish wrapped in brown paper. Before he turned to go, he spoke the prophetic word, 'This is all you will need.' The word was so unlikely, so powerful and unpredictable, and it came as a shaft of hope. There was no denying that God knew our situation and was with us in it.

Utterances and impressions

The emerging prophet will find that frequently the word comes as an utterance, as illustrated above, and this was a prominent feature of Israel's prophets. Amos exclaims, 'The LORD roars from Zion and thunders from Jerusalem; the pastures of the shepherds dry up, and the top of Carmel withers' (Amos 1:2). And again, 'Hear this word of the LORD . . . "You only have I chosen of all the families of the earth; therefore I will punish you for all your sins"' (3:1–2).

Haggai encourages the struggling nation by speaking the Lord's words, 'I am with you', and this utterance is followed by a powerful move of the Holy Spirit, which galvanizes the nation and its leaders into action (see Haggai 1:13).

When such words are given, it is God's expectation that

the prophet will speak them out. It is important, however, that we are sensitive and choose the right situation in which to speak. Any lack of sensitivity can be a hindrance to a person receiving the word.

There will be occasions when you are certain of the word to give, such as the time I told my friend that the Lord was calling him into full-time ordained Christian ministry. There will be other situations, however, in which the insight is not so clear. At a conference I was standing next to a man in his thirties during a period of worship. As I glanced at him, I had an inward sense that God was calling him to work full time with young people. There was no word, just an impression, so when I spoke to him I asked in the context of a normal conversation whether he had ever contemplated working with young people. I made no reference to God or his calling. The man indicated that he had been thinking about this, and I then suggested that it could well be the way that God was calling him.

Times and dates

Most of us will have had Jehovah's Witnesses at our doors heralding the end of the world, which they say will take place on a certain date. I have managed to live through several of these final dates, which they have been announcing since my youth. It is essential that, as emerging Christian prophets, we never give dates regarding the fulfilment of a word that we believe God has given us.

Sadly, in some charismatic circles, certain leaders have given dates relating to the coming of revival in the UK. I have no doubt at all that revival will come, but the dates given have already come and gone, and this has not helped the integrity of the prophetic movement.

The prophetic word is like a time bomb. As soon as it is

spoken, a divine clock is set in motion that will tick away until God's appointed time. When we think of time in Scripture in relation to the fulfilment of prophecy, we find that there are few actual times given. With reference to the fall of Moab, Isaiah says 'within three years' (Isaiah 16:13); of the fall of Kedar he says 'within one year', and he foretells the coming of a drought to Israel 'in little more than a year'. Within 65 years Ephraim would be judged (7:8), and the judgement of Tyre would last for 70 years. In nearly all these predictions, the exact time is veiled.

Definite times are few and far between. In a dream Abraham is told that his descendants will be held in slavery in Egypt for 400 years, and Jeremiah and others give the time the nation will spend in Babylon as 70 years (see Jeremiah 25:11).

It is notable that Isaiah's prophecies concerning the coming of the Messiah ticked away for 700 years. Joseph's dreams waited for 25 years, and Jesus' prophecy concerning the destruction of the Temple in Jerusalem waited for 37 years.

Throughout the books of the prophets there are repeated phrases which surround the prophetic utterances. One of the most commonly used is 'the days are coming', and another phrase is 'in that day'. It is important that we do not stray away from these phrases when considering the fulfilment of our own prophecies.

Above all, it is vital to understand that the prophetic word creates hope for change, but this does not happen automatically. First it must be received, and then it must be acted upon.

6

God Is Speaking

In the past God spoke to our forefathers through the prophets at many times and in various ways. (Hebrews 1:1)

In this chapter I want to take a look at what could be described as the 'miscellaneous' ways in which God speaks to the emerging prophet. These include parables, visions, supernatural sounds, families, allusion to past places and experiences, creation, natural disasters, and riddles.

Parables

I will open my mouth in parables,
I will utter hidden things,
things from of old.
(Psalm 78:2)

Through the prophet Hosea the Lord speaks to Judah and Israel, underlining the fact that, although he has spoken to them, they have ignored him. 'I spoke to the prophets, gave them many visions and told parables through them' (Hosea 12:10).

The Jewish prophets used the term 'parable' in the broadest and most inclusive way. For them it encompassed poems, plays, pictures and symbols. They took one thing and made it resemble something else. God draws on all sorts of things to make his ways known, and we often find that profound truth comes to us in simple ways.

In many incidents in the Old Testament God appears as a lawyer: what he says is very precise and he speaks the law. This law is immediately understandable and enforceable. The Ten Commandments as given to Moses were not part of a document for discussion; they were laws to be obeyed.

Through parables God gives his word a cultural context, speaking into the here and now and involving us in a way to which we can relate. The parables separate the seeker of truth from the know-all of religion and are for those who truly want to be informed and obedient to him. Parables can speak directly to the imagination – and what the Holy Spirit is seeking to develop in the emerging prophet is a prophetic imagination.

The overriding meaning of the word 'parable' is 'things put side by side'. By activating the listener's imagination in describing one thing, the parable reveals another truth that cannot so easily be discovered by the rational mind.

Jesus' most famous parable concerns a sower, and it is as if he sees the scene in his imagination as he speaks to the crowd. In his teaching through parables Matthew claims that Jesus is fulfilling the prophetic word (see Matthew 13:35). Jesus imagines a farmer walking across a field broadcasting seed. The seed falls in a variety of places (see Mark 4:1ff), some on a pathway that crosses the field, some on rocky ground where the soil is shallow, and some among thorns. Much also falls on good, fertile soil. The growth of the seed depends on which type of soil it lands on. The positive application concerns the seed that grows and matures in the fertile soil. Here one seed reproduces itself 40, 60 and even 100 times.

Jesus later says that this is like his word of life being sown on the hearts of different people, from whom there are a variety of responses. He is emphasizing that things you can see in the natural illustrate things you cannot see in the spiritual. In this parable we are being introduced to the most profound truth concerning Jesus and his word. It is only to his disciples that Jesus interprets this parable, however. He leaves the Holy Spirit to make the interpretation to others whom he seeks to bring into a place of faith. He just speaks out the parable that his Father has brought to his imagination. The parable acts like a window: on looking through it you can see and hear the word from God.

Parables for an individual

Sometimes a prophet is given a parable to speak to an individual. Nathan prophesied in the days of King David. The king was at the height of his power when the Lord gave Nathan a parable to speak to him. The Lord had seen David commit adultery with a young woman named Bathsheba. He had tried to cover up the evil he had done by arranging for her husband Uriah to be killed in battle.

The Lord revealed the facts to Nathan about what had happened, and it would have been logical for the prophet to confront the king directly with what had been revealed to him. Instead he received a revelation telling him to speak to David in the form of a parable. Nathan duly sought an audience with the king and spoke the revelation to him in the form which the Lord had given to him. He told David the story of two men, one exceedingly rich and the other poor. The poor man had a little ewe lamb that he loved dearly. When a traveller came by asking for hospitality from the rich man, instead of providing from his own numerous flocks, the rich man took the poor man's lamb and had it slaughtered for the meal.

As David heard the parable unfold, he burned with anger. He proclaimed that the man who had done such a wicked thing deserved to die, or at the very least should pay back four times the cost of the ewe.

What follows is probably one of the most heroic prophetic statements ever made, considering that David was at the height of his power and influence. Nathan said simply to David, 'You are the man.' Then he confronted him with the facts of his adultery and the death of Uriah (see 2 Samuel 12:1ff).

The parable was the window through which David received conviction of sin. In such circumstances it is essential that the emerging prophet speaks exactly what he is given in the parable. Nathan had the advantage of knowing what the situation was into which he was speaking, but there may be times when we are called upon to speak a parable into a situation of which we have no prior knowledge.

Once I was invited by a group of churches in the north of France to lead a gathering for young people in the city of Lille. I went with our youth pastor Mike Pilavachi, who subsequently founded the national youth movement Soul Survivor. Mike was very much in a transition period at that time. He had, in fact, just resigned from the post of youth pastor at St Andrew's, Chorleywood, and was about to start his new venture.

Mike comes to terms with new situations by talking about them incessantly, and during our drive to Lille we had a constant repeat of the following conversation. Mike kept saying that he had made an incredible mistake in resigning as pastor of the young people at our church. He kept hoping that I would agree with him, that somehow everything could be reversed and he could take up his old position again. Each time he said this I replied, 'You've grown out of an old ministry, and the Lord is releasing you into a new one.'

Eventually we arrived at Lille, found the hall and met those who were organizing the conference. In the middle of the room there was a large table set for a meal, and we were invited to sit. As neither Mike nor I speak French, we both had interpreters, and during the excellent meal we planned the format and content of the weekend. At the end of the meal it was suggested that we have a time of worship, and a young pastor picked up his guitar and started to lead us.

After some time an older man left the table and walked across the hall. I watched him pick up a coat obviously left by a three- or four-year-old child, then he came back to the table and stood behind Mike. He proceeded to try to put the little coat on Mike. He started to push Mike's right hand into the sleeve, but of course it was completely impossible to make the coat fit. The prophet then spoke. 'You've grown out of an old ministry,' he said, 'and the Lord is releasing you into a new one.' These were the exact words I had spoken to Mike many times on our journey to Lille. The parable of Mike trying to get into this little coat was a window through which he could see the spiritual truth that the Lord was showing him.

For nearly two decades I have had the privilege of teaching once or twice a year at the YWAM base in Amsterdam. On one occasion I was preparing to go when I heard the Lord distinctly say that I should take a lectern with me and present it to the base. This seemed very illogical, because the community already had many lecterns in their lecture rooms. The one I was to give was very heavy and angular. I was able to take it apart to a certain extent, but it was still extremely difficult to carry.

On the morning of my departure, I arrived at Heathrow airport with the lectern. I was not able to check it in at the normal place, so I had to walk the length of Terminal One to a special parcel reception desk. On the way I knocked into numerous people and laddered someone's tights. By the time I had deposited my parcel, I had said 'sorry' to nearly every person I had met.

The arrival at Schiphol airport was no different. It took an inordinate amount of time to relocate the lectern and carry it to meet my hosts. They were incredibly surprised to see the awkward package. I did not tell them what it was, and they were too polite to ask. I took the lectern straight to my room and hid it in a corner, wondering why on earth I had brought it.

On the Wednesday evening I was invited to speak to the whole community. As I prepared to speak, I felt that the Lord wanted me to take the lectern, unwrap it and then present it to the community. When the time came, I took a sharp knife and cut away the binding. While everyone watched curiously, I assembled the lectern, then stood behind it and rested my notes on it. As I did this, the word came: 'This lectern is a symbol from which the good news of Jesus is preached. I want you to take this gospel to the nations.'

This had always been the call upon the young people who joined YWAM, and the bases on all the continents existed to facilitate such a task. At times, however, an initial vision can grow dim and those involved can forget what they have been called to do. For the YWAM base in Amsterdam, this prophetic action and word led to a renewal of the original vision.

Parables for a nation

As we have seen, there are parables in which God is speaking through the prophet to an individual, but there are also parables in which he is speaking to the church and the nation.

On one occasion Jeremiah was told by the Lord to go down to the potter's house. Once he was there, the Lord would show him the message (see Jeremiah 18:1ff). When Jeremiah arrived at the house he stood and watched the potter working. He noticed that if the pot were marred in any way, the potter would simply start again with the clay and form it into another shape. Here Jeremiah received a huge message in a simple picture. An object of daily experience became an object of prophetic significance. The Lord was saying to him that in his eyes the nation was marred because of its evil ways. If the people repented, however, the Lord would, like the potter, start again with them.

Some parables that the Lord speaks to the prophet will offer insight into the will and immediate purposes of God. The year 587 BC was one of the most traumatic in Jewish history. The words of the prophets reached their fulfilment in the exiling of the middle and upper classes of the Jewish nation to Babylon. Jeremiah was left behind with the remnant of the people. He wondered to himself what the future held for the divided nation. As he walked by the Temple, the Lord drew his attention to two baskets of figs (see Jeremiah 24:1ff). As he looked at them, the Lord asked him what he was seeing, and Jeremiah replied that one of the baskets contained good and edible figs, while the other was full of figs that had rotted. The Lord then applied the parable. The good figs represented those of the nation who had gone into Babylon. The Lord promised to watch over them and bring them back to the land having experienced an inner transformation. The poor figs represented those in rebellion, and the judgement of God rested upon them.

The 17th October 1987 will always be a date I remember. I had risen early and was taking our cocker spaniel Ziggy for her regular walk up the nearby Chess Valley. That particular walk took an hour and ran through farmland, along a narrow country lane and back through a mature forest. As the forest came into view, I stopped dead, staring in absolute amazement and incredulity. Of the entire forest, hardly one tree was standing. The rest were lying scattered around the hillside as if the contents of some gigantic box of matches had been tipped on the ground. The previous night a hurricane had struck the south coast and caused terrible devastation. It had not been predicted – indeed, in an action that has now passed into television mythology, the weatherman Michael Fish had publicly denied that any hurricane might be pending.

As I stood taking in the situation, I heard the inner, audible voice of God say to me, 'I am about to shake the nations and the church.' The following month, the whole of Europe as we knew it began to be shaken apart. Political boundaries and regional spheres of authority that had been set up at the Yalta Conference 40 years previously were swept away. Communism disappeared almost overnight. As with the hurricane, God swept across nations in a way that astonished onlookers.

I believe that a similar shaking of the church has also started, as God addresses not political boundaries but spiritual strongholds. Such a parable is rooted in reality. The trees were real objects in the material world, but what I saw was a symbol of a spiritual truth. The image of devastated trees was a window into the spiritual world. Through them I was seeing beyond time and space. In a similar way, while he is teaching about the end of the world and the signs that will herald it, Jesus points out a fig tree (see Mark 14:28). He reminds his listeners that when they see leaves start to form, they know summer is just around the corner. In the same way, when they observe the signs he has outlined, they will know that his Second Coming is near.

Parables in song

Parables can sometimes be conveyed in song. Isaiah sang a song to the nation concerning a vineyard (see Isaiah 5:1ff). His theme was that the person he loved owned a vineyard located on a fertile hillside. This person cleared the location of stones and planted the best vines. To guard it against thieves he erected a watchtower, and in preparation for the harvest he made a winepress. When the time to harvest approached he went out into the vineyard, but discovered only bad fruit. He addressed the nation, asking them to make a judgement. He had done everything possible to guarantee a good harvest.

Then came the application. The Lord's 'vineyard' was the houses of Israel and Judah, and he delighted in them. Then he looked for the fruits of justice and righteousness, but found only bloodshed and distress.

Questions answered by parable

Often God answers the deep questionings of the prophet through a parable. When Jeremiah was called by God as a young man, he was told of an impending judgement that was about to come on the nation (see Jeremiah 1:1ff). In this he would have a significant part to play as he spoke God's words of warning to the nation.

On one occasion, Jeremiah was walking in the countryside wondering whether the message of judgement that he was giving would ever be fulfilled. The Lord, knowing his deepest thoughts, drew his attention to the branch of an almond tree and asked him what he saw. Jeremiah described the almond branch. The Lord then told him that he was watching over his word to fulfil it. In this revelation there is a subtle association of ideas: in Hebrew the word for 'almond branch' is *saked* and the word for 'watching' is *sakad*. This would not have been lost on the young prophet. God was telling him that just as the almond tree would bear fruit, so would the word which God had given him to speak, because God himself was watching over it. The ideas are put side by side as a parable.

Other aspects also apparently troubled Jeremiah. He wondered how the judgement would come to pass, and through whom. Again the Lord asked him what he was seeing. He replied that he was watching a boiling pot, which was tilting away from the north. From this the Lord indicated that the impending judgement would come from that direction.

Visions

When a prophet of the Lord is among you,
I reveal myself to him in visions.
(Numbers 12:6)

Some revelations from God are received through visions. The words 'dream' and 'vision' come from the same Hebrew root meaning 'to see'. The two forms of revelation are different, but both show images and film-like pictures moving in the mind or before the eyes. Sometimes during a dream a vision is also given – the dream being like a film which passes from scene to scene, while the accompanying vision appears as a still picture.

Nebuchadnezzar relates this experience to the prophet

Daniel: 'I had a dream that made me afraid. As I was lying in my bed, the images and visions that passed through my mind terrified me' (Daniel 4:5). In the same book, a similar experience is recorded for the prophet: 'Daniel had a dream, and visions passed through his mind as he was lying on his bed' (7:1).

In the New Testament, Paul has a vision during the night of a man from Macedonia who asks him and his team to go to that region and help them (see Acts 16:9). In similar ways on a number of occasions he also sees the Lord (see Acts 18:9; 23:11; 27:23).

Cornelius, a Roman centurion, is praying when he too has a vision in which he distinctly sees an angel (see Acts 10:3). The angel affirms his relationship with God and tells him to send a deputation to the coastal town of Joppa to bring back the man 'Simon who is called Peter'. Cornelius is also given specific instructions in the vision that Simon Peter is staying with a man called Simon the Tanner.

Having a vision or dream might be described as fading from reality for a period of time while we are totally caught up in the visionary experience. It might also be called a trance. Simon Peter – to whom the centurion sent the deputation – also had a vision, and we are told that he received it while he was in a trance (see Acts 10:10). He describes seeing a large sheet being let down from heaven to earth by its four corners, containing all kinds of unclean animals and reptiles. The Lord instructs Peter to kill and eat these animals, but he refuses on the grounds of their impurity. He then hears the voice of the Lord saying that he has made the animals clean. This vision is repeated three times and is key in preparing Peter for meeting with the Gentiles.

Visions can be received both externally and internally. The external vision is seen apart from yourself in three dimensions, in some ways transporting you into the situation you see. The internal vision is like watching a film in your mind, with images and pictures appearing in the imagination.

An external vision

When I was co-hosting the New Wine conference, we would always stay on a farm near the showground. Each morning at six o'clock I would go on a prayer walk for an hour. This took me up a valley, over a high hill and back to the farm.

One evening I was leading the ministry in the main pavilion when I was transported back into the valley. I could see the whole scene in front of me, in three dimensions. Standing at the head of the valley, I looked down and saw a lion in prime condition, sleek, with a bushy mane. He started bounding towards me and he was absolutely free; nothing could restrain him. I heard a voice which kept repeating, 'The Lion of Judah is free.'

As I watched this vision I realized that the Lion of Judah was the risen Jesus, and I found myself saying over and over again, 'The Lion of Judah is free.' When I came back to the reality of the meeting, it was just like waking from a dream. As this external vision had been so vivid and real to me, I was able to minister with the words that the risen Jesus really was free and that he was able to enter powerfully into every situation represented by the people in the gathering.

An internal vision

Normally the visions we receive are internal, coming as pictures in the imagination. In 1 Kings we read how Ahab the king of Israel formed a coalition with Jehoshaphat, the king of Judah, to take back the city of Ramoth Gilead which the king of Aram had annexed. Before the battle, Ahab consulted 400 of his prophets. To a man they all encouraged him to enter the battle, saying that the Lord would give the king of Aram into their hands. Jehoshaphat was not entirely certain of this and asked if 'a prophet of the LORD' could be consulted (1 Kings 22:7). Micaiah the prophet was summoned and was cynical of the wisdom given by the other 400 prophets. When pushed by Ahab, he said, 'I saw all Israel scattered on the hills like sheep without a shepherd' (22:17).

The interpretation of a vision

When you see a vision, it is important to speak exactly what you are seeing and then wait for the interpretation. On one occasion I saw the following vision while leading a service of worship. The vision was situated in New Zealand in a paddock near a farmhouse. This paddock was overgrown with grass and weeds. The area was fenced with wooden posts but behind them, surrounding the paddock, were macrocarpa trees.

As I looked I could see that a young man had been in the paddock for some time. Anxieties and worries imprisoned him there. I was drawn back to the gate, which had been forced open. As I watched, the young man was able to move into the freedom beyond the confines of the paddock. This was the interpretation and it came as an immediate extension of the vision.

My first inclination was to adapt what I saw to an English situation. A macrocarpa tree is a large coniferous tree of New Zealand and is used for shelter belts on farms and for rough timber. I didn't think anyone at the meeting would have any idea what a macrocarpa tree was. I quickly adjusted what I saw to an English situation. The macrocarpa became pine, the paddock became a field and the wooden posts became concrete. I was just about to share the vision in this way when I sensed the Lord say, 'That is not what I showed you.'

I told the vision just as I had seen it. Later a young man came to see me. He was filled with incredulity. What I had described was the paddock next to his family's farmhouse in New Zealand where he had been brought up. He said that he was certainly the person filled with anxiety and fear. Through prayer he was able to be released out of the paddock and into the freedom of the surrounding farmland.

Such a vision gives an incredible affirmation to those for whom it is intended. It means that without doubt the Lord knows a very real and significant situation in their life. The implication is that if he knows that, he obviously knows everything.

On other occasions, you may hear an internal, audible voice at the same time as you see the vision, which will interpret what you have seen. A nine-year-old girl told me the following story. At a meeting she had been overwhelmed by the Holy Spirit and had fallen to the floor. As she lay there, in her imagination she saw a vivid picture of a golden carriage being drawn by four white horses. As she watched this vision, a person was helped into the carriage and taken to heaven. She realized that someone was going to die. In this Holy Spirit-induced experience, she stood up and saw that the person being put into the carriage was her mother. She then heard a voice say, 'Don't worry, your mother is going to heaven.' The reality was that this little girl's mother was in the last stages of terminal cancer. The girl told me how peaceful she had become about her mother's situation. She was still obviously very sad, but she knew that Jesus was about to take her mother to himself. She was given a vision and its interpretation, and it came to her as a sovereign act of God.

Supernatural sounds

> I have heard the sound of the trumpet;
> I have heard the battle cry.
> (Jeremiah 4:19)

There will be times when the emerging prophet will hear such supernatural sounds, and even make them.

On the 11th March 1987 I was speaking at a YWAM conference in Heidebeek in the Netherlands. The meeting that evening was being held in a large hall with a tin roof, and about 400 people were due to attend from the surrounding area.

During the conference I was staying with my friend Bart Dornweerd, who was hosting the conference, and we walked to the meeting. The snows had come and the ploughs had just cleared the road, leaving great banks of snow on either side. Everything was frozen, even the snow that had fallen on the trees. As we walked, I said jokingly that it would be great to have a ladder so that I could climb up and catch a star from the clear sky.

I spoke that night on Elijah and the contest he had with the prophets of Baal on Mount Carmel (see 1 Kings 18:1ff). After the fire of God had fallen on the sacrifice that Elijah had offered, the prophet said to King Ahab, 'Go, eat and drink, for there is the sound of a heavy rain' (18:41). As he spoke, the country was still suffering from the three-year drought that Elijah had initially prophesied. The sky was clear, the sun a flaming ball of unremitting heat.

Elijah had heard a supernatural sound. This was prophetic. In my talk in Heidebeek I made the point that although the church was in a drought-like situation, the rains of the Spirit would surely come and the drought would end. I had just spoken these words when the rain came. I could hear water pelting on the tin roof. I could not believe my ears. How was it possible that rain could come on such a frozen evening? I was right: the rain had not come literally, but the sound of it was a sign of what was to come through the Spirit. It was significant that half the people present did not hear a thing.

Adam and Eve heard the 'sound of the Lord' (Genesis 3:8), and when the Arameans laid siege to Samaria, the Lord caused them 'to hear the sound of chariots and horses and a great army' (2 Kings 7:6). The Lord gave David a sign so that he should know when to attack the Philistines: 'As soon as you hear the sound of marching in the tops of the balsam trees, move quickly' (2 Samuel 5:24).

On one occasion I was speaking at a celebration in Norwich Cathedral. At the ministry time I found myself quite spontaneously whistling into the microphone. This had happened on a number of previous occasions in public meetings. As I did this, I sensed an anointing of the Holy Spirit and saw that many people seemed to have been affected in some way by the whistling. Some unbelievers present sensed that they were being drawn to Christ. Both Zechariah and Isaiah mention this phenomenon. The word for 'whistle' in Hebrew is *sharaq*. In the context of the Lord renewing his people, Zechariah writes, 'Their children will see it and be joyful; their hearts will rejoice in the LORD. I will [whistle] for them and gather them in' (Zechariah 10:7–8). Isaiah writes of the Lord, 'He lifts up a banner for the distant nations, he whistles for those at the ends of the earth' (Isaiah 5:26).

Families

We are signs and symbols in Israel. (Isaiah 8:18)

What happens to emerging prophets and their families is a

message to the church and the nation. The prophet Isaiah was married and his wife was known as a prophetess. They had two sons. The elder of these boys was Shear-Jashub, a name given by God that means 'a remnant will return' (Isaiah 7:3) – the sign being that there was a coming judgement. The nation would go into exile, but in the future a group would return.

The Lord then told Isaiah to write the name Maher-Shalal-Hash-Baz on a large scroll with an ordinary pen. This name meant 'quick to the plunder, swift to the spoil' (8:3). He was to ask Uriah the priest and Zechariah to witness what he had done. Shortly afterwards, Isaiah's wife conceived and gave birth to a son. At the birth the Lord told him to name the boy Maher-Shalal-Hash-Baz. It was a sign that before the little boy learned to speak, the king of Assyria would have invaded and plundered both Samaria and Damascus.

The prophet Hosea was asked by the Lord to marry Diblaim's daughter Gomer, who was a prostitute and adulterer. This marriage symbolized to the nation how God viewed his relationship with Israel, who had prostituted herself with other gods. Hosea was to call his first son Jezreel, after a city where Jehu had massacred the royal family. This little boy was a sign to the nation that the Lord would judge the house of Jehu. Hosea was then to call his only daughter Lo-Ruhamah, which means 'not loved'. This was to be a sign that the Lord would no longer show his love to Israel. Finally, he was to call his youngest son Lo-Ammi, meaning 'not my people'. He was a sign that the Lord had rejected Israel.

During the last six years, Mary and I have come to see something of the prophetic significance associated with our family, as overnight we added four wonderful young people to our number. On the 23rd August 1996, the doorbell rang. Standing on the front doorstep with our youth worker Will Kemp were four very traumatized and frightened young people. A few hours earlier, their father had murdered their mother. Although the family had worshipped at our church some months before, they had since left to join another church and I had never had a conversation with the children, our only contact being a mutual greeting as they left a service.

We took them in and Mary made them breakfast. As she did so, we wondered whom out of our kind and loving congregation I could ask to look after them. We soon realized that it would be wrong to split them up, but who could accommodate four young people? Later that day Mary suggested that, until other arrangements could be made, they should stay with us. Somehow we managed to fit them into our home, but it was quite a squash.

The young people were still with us three weeks later, and I felt it was probably time to make some more permanent arrangements. As I discussed this with Mary, she looked at me and said, 'Barry, I think the Lord is telling me that we should become their foster parents and have them living with us. Permanently.'

I was shaken. For one thing, it definitely did not fit in with what I saw as the answer to recent prayers about our future. Mary and I were not going to be travelling together very far with a traumatized twelve-year-old girl to look after. Anyway, I felt it had been hard enough bringing my own three children through their teenage years, and the idea of repeating it again with four young people I hardly knew filled me with apprehension. I told Mary that we needed to wait before such a decision was made. In the short time that they had been with us, I had come to love the children, but I did not see us having a long-term involvement with them. It hardly fitted with our plans.

Nonetheless, God overruled me.

Given the circumstances surrounding the death of the children's mother, we realized that it was going to take a long time before the coroner could release the body. Together we decided to have an initial service of thanksgiving in our church and to follow this up later with a service at the crematorium. At the service of thanksgiving, I saw what an incredible family these children were. Each one wrote an appreciation of their mother's life and read it during the service. Never, it seemed, had their faith in Jesus wavered, and in those initial days of loss and trauma they quietly drew strength from reading the Scriptures and praying. Their mother had been a committed Christian and had obviously imparted to each of her children a deep and real faith. Unknown to us all, this faith was going to be tested yet further. They too would be struck by the storm that was soon to break over us.

Their mother's body was eventually released and we were able to prepare for the service at the crematorium. I suggested that the children write a letter to their mother and say the things they would have wanted to say if they'd had the chance. In the chapel of the crematorium we stood together round the coffin. I read a short scripture on the hope of the resurrection and said a simple prayer. I then invited the family to place their letters on the coffin and say anything they wanted to say.

As they were doing this, I heard Jesus speak to me in an audible voice. 'Today, I give you this family to parent and care for.'

Tears started to stream down my face and I began to sob deeply. Questions flooded my mind: How could I possibly have the resources for such a task? Could this be part of the Lord's will in response to the recommitment of my life?

I knew I had to make a response to God's voice. I sobbed

back my answer: 'Yes Lord, if you will be my helper.'

Their family is now our family, and our family is now their family. This is the message: In the days to come there will be such a turning to Jesus that the churches will be full of people who are not from our background or culture – but for this great move of God to proceed, we will have to welcome them unreservedly into our church family. God speaks through the emerging prophet and his family.

Allusion to past places and experiences

The emerging prophet may see a panoramic view of the ways in which God speaks and works with his people. Places of the past are often given prophetic significance in the present. For example, the Lord said through Hosea that he would make the Valley of Achor a 'door of hope' (Hosea 2:15). In the past the Valley of Achor had been a place of judgement. It had been a valley of trouble, and Achan and his family were stoned there for stealing and lying. Now, however, it was to be a door of hope (see Joshua 7:26).

The prophet will often take an event that has already happened in a certain place, or in the past, and reinterpret it with a contemporary significance.

Creation

> The heavens declare the glory of God.
> (Psalm 19:1)

The prophet hears God speaking through every aspect of creation. Climatic conditions can be a symbol of the workings of God's Spirit. Hosea, for example, sees that God will come 'like the winter rains, like the spring rains that water the earth' (Hosea 6:3). After the Spirit of God has broken into the hardness of a man's heart, Hosea sees that he will come like rain to soften it. He also sees that when the seed of the word of God is sown in a man's heart, the Spirit will come to make it grow.

Through the plants and trees, Hosea hears God's voice. While he observes the vineyard and vines, God speaks to him and tells him that his church is like a spreading vine (Hosea 10:1). It is also like an olive tree and a cedar of Lebanon (14:6). God also uses birds and animals as vehicles of his word, showing Ephraim as a dove, in this instance meaning 'easily deceived and senseless' (7:11). Hosea also sees the eagle over the house of God as a sign of judgement (8:1).

I was recently helping one of my daughters move into her new flat in Putney. It had been raining very heavily and there were floods spreading across the country, causing much heartache and millions of pounds of damage. The rain continued to pour down as I waited outside the flat by the van. Then an old lady emerged from an alleyway. She was elegantly dressed and was trying to shield herself from the rain with a large umbrella. As she passed me, I made some inane comment about the weather and she stopped, gathered herself together, and said simply, 'The Lord is speaking, but no one is listening.' I could only nod in agreement, realizing that this was indeed a prophetic word. God speaks through the weather; it just remains to be seen whether we will hear his voice.

At all times the emerging prophet should observe creation and listen for the voice of God. This may come through any aspect of what God has created. When this happens, there will be an inward pull towards an aspect of what you are seeing. The Spirit of the Lord will ask, 'What do you see?' and when you look, the thoughts of the Holy Spirit will start to fill your mind.

Natural disasters

The emerging prophet will also start to hear the voice of God in what are termed 'natural disasters'. The prophet Joel vividly heard the word of God through a swarm of locusts. This swarm invaded the land, causing terrible devastation, and they were like an army that would invade the nation bringing the Lord's judgement (see Joel 1).

Riddles

In Psalm 49 David says, 'With the harp I will expound my riddle' (v. 4), and the word 'riddle' means 'a play upon words'. A classic example of this is found in the opening chapter of Micah. The place names in this section have extra, hidden meanings that are used to make a point. Thus the following phrases become riddles: 'tell it not in Gath' ('Gath' means 'tell'); 'in Beth Ophrah . . . roll in the dust' ('Beth Ophrah' means 'house of dust'); 'those who live in Zaanan . . . will not come out' ('Zaanan' means 'come out'); 'you who live in Lachish . . . harness the team to the chariot' ('Lachish' means 'team'); 'the town of Aczib . . . will prove deceptive' ('Aczib' means 'deception').

One of our young men from the church was going to work in a hospital in Africa. As a leadership we prayed with him before he went, and while we were doing this I heard the Lord say, 'The piece of string will be neither too long nor too short.' This was a riddle, and the obvious meaning was that for the journey he would have neither too much nor too little, but the Lord had promised him everything he needed. When he returned, he said how encouraging and how right the riddle had been.

When you receive a riddle, it is best to speak it out and not try to analyse what it may or may not mean. When I first spoke out this riddle, I felt a bit foolish as I had no idea of its meaning or application – but it was indeed a much-needed word from the Lord.

7

The Prophet in the Congregation

> Do not put out the Spirit's fire; do not treat prophecies with
> contempt. (1 Thessalonians 5:19)

It is within the worshipping congregation that the emerging prophet has the opportunity of bringing the word of
God to the people. From Paul's first letter to the church in
Corinth we see that it is God's intention to speak to his
gathered people through his prophets. For this to happen
in a way that will edify and build up the church, the leadership needs to provide structures in which the prophetic
can be expressed. This is the key to prophetic expression
within a congregation, and in this chapter we shall consider the relevant structures.

From the outset it is necessary to understand that the
prophet's contribution is only a part of the ministry of the
word of God. First, it is important that the Scriptures,
which contain everything needful for salvation, are read.
Whatever the theme of the worship, readings that illustrate
this should come from both the Old and New Testaments.
Second, the word of God comes to the congregation
through the preaching and teaching of it. Such preaching is
again biblically based. Third, it is necessary for the congre-

gation to hear what God has been doing in the lives of those who gather to worship. Through testimony people can share how the word of God has changed their lives in certain respects. Finally, there is the inspired word spoken to the people by the prophets. For a church to be healthy, all these means of receiving God's word should be in operation. There should also be opportunity for personal prayer as the word of God opens up new possibilities for his people.

The challenge to congregational prophecy comes through Paul's teaching on the gifts of the Spirit in 1 Corinthians 12–14. Having named nine particular gifts which the Holy Spirit imparts to believing Christians, he then concentrates on the way in which these should be exercised. In every instance the prophet must be motivated by love for the person or people receiving the prophecies. Each Christian is to 'eagerly desire spiritual gifts, especially the gift of prophecy' (14:1) and should 'be eager to prophesy' (14:39).

The purpose of prophecy

One of Jesus' most profound teachings on communication between himself and the believer is contained in John 10, where he likens himself to the good shepherd and a believer to a sheep. In this teaching there is a mixture of metaphors as Jesus presents himself not only as the good shepherd but also as the gate. The picture is of a sheep pen, the only way into it is through the gate, and the shepherd leads the sheep in and out of the pen. The sheep are characterized by the fact that they listen to the shepherd's voice, which calls them by name, and they respond because they are familiar with that voice.

One of the greatest Christian values is to hear the voice

of the Father who speaks to us through Jesus. When this happens the church is, in Paul's terms, built up through being strengthened, encouraged and comforted (see 1 Corinthians 14:2), and together we know that God is indeed with us.

When we first started to send out Faith Sharing teams from our church at St Andrew's, Chorleywood, in 1974, it was a pioneering ministry. Not many other churches were doing such a thing. Our church council believed that God was leading us to be available in this way, but the rightness of it had to be conveyed to and accepted by the congregation. One of the problems was that of exclusiveness. Certain people, because of their particular gifting, were invited to join and travel with the various teams. This obviously meant that some who would have liked to be involved were not invited.

One Sunday evening there came a prophetic word. Like many such words, although it did not quote a scripture, it had a biblical reference point. The word said that it was the Lord's intention to share his blessing equally between those who travelled with teams and those who stayed at home. King David first expounded this principle when he was leading the battle against the Amalekites, whom he subsequently defeated. On returning from the battle he insisted, 'The share of the man who stayed with the supplies is to be the same as that of him who went down to the battle. All shall share alike' (1 Samuel 30:24).

After this word had been given, many who had been sceptics told me privately that they had been encouraged and it had led to them being more involved locally and interceding for those who travelled with the teams.

Another purpose of such prophecy is so that 'everyone may be instructed and encouraged' (1 Corinthians 14:31). Through the prophetic word, instructions in the ways of

God can be given. On one occasion I had what I believed to be two prophetic messages based on Scripture. For a number of days I prayed, asking the Lord to show me which of these would be appropriate for the following Sunday evening. When it was time to go to the church, I was still in a quandary about what to preach, so I took both the words with me. During the worship, one of our prophets spoke. Her message was a précis of one of the talks that I had prepared. Consequently there came a great anointing on the word and much ministry followed as people sought to obey the instructions of the Lord.

There is also a close connection between significant evangelism and the prophetic word. We have seen this to be the case when a prophet speaks to an individual, speaking from revelation. This can equally be true when the word is spoken to the general congregation and impacts an unbeliever. Paul says that the following can be experienced during worship:

> If an unbeliever or someone who does not understand comes in while everybody is prophesying, he will be convinced by all that he is a sinner and will be judged by all, and the secrets of his heart will be laid bare. So he will fall down and worship God, exclaiming, 'God is really among you!' (1 Corinthians 14:24–25)

A young woman in her twenties came as a visitor to our church. Over a period of many months she had been considering the claims of Jesus Christ, and the more she understood, the more she realized that her whole style of life would have to change if she decided to become a follower of Jesus. For a number of weeks she had tried to put the decision out of her mind, but it was persistently with her. A phrase kept coming into her mind: 'There must be a parting of the ways.' She realized that it could well be God speaking to her.

One Sunday evening she was brought to our church by a friend, and later she said that she had found the talk helpful and had enjoyed the worship. That is, she had enjoyed it until the music stopped and everything went still. Breaking the stillness, she heard a man's voice say, 'Tonight there must be a parting of the ways.' This struck her like an electric shock, and she felt that God was giving her an ultimatum. She saw the stark choice and turned to Jesus for forgiveness and a new life.

Giving and receiving a prophetic word

To speak with authority and conviction, the prophet needs to have an anointing by the Holy Spirit. This is hard to define, but those who are sensitive to the ways of the Spirit will know when this anointing is upon the prophet. This can be experienced in a number of ways.

There is a burden that the Holy Spirit puts upon the prophets, which can often be experienced as a physical weight. They may feel that unless they speak out they will burst, and once the words are spoken they feel a conscious relief.

Often there can be a physical manifestation. Jeremiah writes of his own experiences of the anointing in the following terms. The Lord said to him, 'I will make my words in your mouth a fire and these people the wood it consumes' (Jeremiah 5:14). The prophet writes, 'His words are in my heart like a fire, a fire shut up in my bones. I am weary of holding it in; indeed, I cannot' (20:9). He also says, 'My heart pounds within me, I cannot keep silent' (4:19).

There was a season in our church when the power of

God came on the prophets and they were hardly able to stand, having great difficulty in speaking the word that the Lord had given them. Often their lips would quiver and become hot, their hearts would beat extremely quickly, and they would know a quickening of the Spirit within. There would come upon them an authority and confidence, brought by the inner knowledge that the word they had received had come from God.

In his teaching on congregational prophecy, Paul brings both a warning and a challenge. He writes to the church meeting in Thessalonica, saying, 'Do not put out the Spirit's fire; do not treat prophecies with contempt. Test everything. Hold on to the good' (1 Thessalonians 5:19–21).

One of the major reasons for treating prophecy with contempt is that at times the words may seem trite. On occasions I have heard people say, 'God is saying that he loves you.' When I have heard such words, I have often discarded them because the truth is so obvious and is at the very heart of all we believe about God. When the people returned to Israel from their 70-year exile in Babylon, however, the prophetic word was equally simple. Through Haggai the Lord confronted the people with their lack of commitment to his priorities. They had returned to Israel and, instead of first rebuilding the Temple as their place of worship, they had begun by building their own houses and planting the land. This instance the people listened to Haggai and obeyed the prophetic word, starting to restore the place of worship. As they were engaged in this, Haggai received another word from the Lord. It was simply, 'The Lord says, "I am with you."'

There are many ways in which the prophet will receive words for speaking into the congregation, and God will always speak in a way that the prophet will understand. Sometimes the word will come during the course of the week. There is an interesting account of receiving the word in both Ezekiel and Jeremiah. Ezekiel is presented with a scroll that has writing on both sides. He is handed this and is asked to eat it. He records, 'So I ate it, and it tasted as sweet as honey in my mouth' (Ezekiel 3:1ff). Similarly, addressing the Lord, Jeremiah says, 'When your words came, I ate them; they were my joy and my heart's delight' (Jeremiah 15:16). Both these experiences speak of a process of digestion through which the word needs to go before it is spoken. Such a prophetic word can be like yeast in bread. A word starts to rise within the prophet and impresses itself upon him. Further revelation flows, and the word grows within.

On other occasions the prophet has nothing to bring to the church. During the worship, however, a number of apparently disconnected thoughts begin to come to mind. After some time meditating on these, the prophet is gradually able to understand and arrange them in a coherent order. Once he is confident, he is able to speak the word to the church.

Paul writes to the Christians in Rome, 'If a man's gift is prophesying, let him use it in proportion to his faith' (Romans 12:6). When such prophecy is being received, it often comes like a phrase or sentence written on a scroll. Only as you speak what you see does the rest of the scroll unroll sentence by sentence.

At such times the Holy Spirit may give a prophetic picture that is impressed onto the imagination. This may be self-explanatory, or it may require an interpretation. This interpretation may be given to the prophet receiving the picture, or it may come to another person as it is spoken out. The key to such revelation is the word, which interprets it.

Pitfalls to avoid

When introducing a prophecy, it is important that the emerging prophet does not prefix the prophecy with phrases such as 'this is the word of the Lord', or 'the Lord has shown me this'. Equally, it would be unhelpful to end with a 'thus says the Lord'. Instead the prophetic word needs to be offered humbly, remembering that it is the leaders and congregation who are to weigh and judge that word. The prophet may say something like, 'I think the Lord could be saying this . . .'

There are two pitfalls in particular which emerging prophets will encounter. The first is that they will start with a confident sentence or two and then panic and dry up completely, leaving them feeling rather embarrassed. Or they will speak what the Lord has given and then continue in their own words, not quite knowing how to finish. They start in revelation and end up in perspiration! The embarrassment is then upon the congregation. The key is to listen to the Holy Spirit and keep speaking until the anointing and thoughts you initially received have finished. Then stop, and do not try to add your own thoughts.

Sifting the received word

Once you sense that you have received a word from the Lord, it is necessary to apply a number of criteria. The first one is to examine your own life in the light of what you have heard and ask yourself whether the word you have received is for you personally. Often the word is not put through this initial filter, and the word is spoken over the congregation. As soon as it is heard, those who discern such things will immediately know that it is God's word to the prophet and not to the congregation.

God has seasons in which, through his Spirit, he is doing certain things, and the prophet will have access to this information. With this in mind, Amos wrote, 'Surely the Sovereign LORD does nothing without revealing his plan to his servants the prophets' (Amos 3:7). This means that in certain situations a particular word will come often to a prophet. On one occasion I was with a team touring New Zealand and we were invited to minister in a church in Whangarei. After I had spoken on the Sunday morning, my wife Mary heard the Lord say clearly, 'Don't worry about my church, I am raising up a secret army.' This was a word which came to her often in a variety of situations. In the days ahead, I travelled to a variety of churches in different nations and also heard the same word.

Often during worship the prophet will receive revelation highlighting a condition in someone's life to which the Lord wants to minister. This is not something to be given as a prophecy, but instead should be given at another, more appropriate time. In many congregations there is an opportunity to speak out this type of word at the end of the worship or during a ministry time.

Overseeing the prophetic ministry

In the local congregation the prophet will always function under the authority of the senior pastor or minister. It is the minister who has the God-given authority to lead and take responsibility for all that happens during the act of worship. In the churches with which I have been involved, we have found it helpful to lay down the following structure for those with a prophetic ministry. This also creates faith, trust and confidence within the congregation.

The structure only permits church members to offer prophetic words. This is not only to protect the church, but also to make the prophet accountable for the words that are spoken. It also gives the pastor the opportunity to discuss the prophecy with the prophet if need be, and to teach and encourage him or her in the ministry.

When introducing this ministry to the congregation, the pastor needs much patience with the emerging prophets. At times they may get things wrong. It is important that nothing negative or critical is said publicly, only privately and in an attitude of encouragement.

In his writing on this subject, Paul infers that one prophetic period is limited to two or at most three contributions. He says, 'Two or three prophets should speak' (1 Corinthians 14:29). These words can be received in a number of ways, depending on the size of the congregation and the acoustics of the building. In a small gathering the prophets can stand and speak from their seats, and as they do so the pastor can précis each prophecy, repeating it for those who may not have heard it.

In a larger gathering it is advisable for the prophet to come to the front and share with the pastor what he or she intends to say. The pastor will then decide whether the prophet should give the word over the microphone, or whether the pastor should speak it to the congregation instead. After the prophetic words have been given, it is important that the congregation spends time in silence contemplating what they have heard.

It is very helpful to have such a structure, but, like all things pertaining to the Holy Spirit, there will be exceptions and both the pastor and the prophet need to be listening to the Lord. On one occasion I was leading an annual gathering in a marquee on our local common to which local churches came. Each weeknight we had a visiting speaker. One evening prior to the meeting I had a telephone call from Nicolas Rivet-Carnac, who was then the

vicar of St Mark's, Kennington. He said he had been praying for us and felt that the Lord had spoken to him about
that particular evening. He sensed that the Lord was going
to send to the meeting a prophet to speak a word to the
gathering, and although I would not normally have
allowed this, I was to make an exception this time. As an
aside he also indicated that the appearance of the person
concerned would make me defensive and rejecting.

The worship was inspiring, and we came to the point
when a prophetic word could have been appropriate. I
waited in silence until a strange-looking man came forward from the back. He said he had a word from God for
the gathering. The terminology would normally have put
me off, but because of Nicolas's word I handed him the
microphone. He spoke an incredible word concerning
God's heart for the suffering of the poor. Extraordinarily,
when our visiting speaker introduced his subject, it was
the same as the prophet's. Afterwards many people were
touched, and years later some are still financially support-
ing families in India as a direct result of that word.

Evaluating prophecy

Paul is insistent that the words spoken are 'weighed' or
tested carefully (1 Corinthians 14:29). This is done in a
variety of ways. They should be weighed by the prophets,
then by the pastor, and finally by the congregation. Each
one must listen to the spirit in which it is given and the
words must 'follow the way of love'. They must
strengthen, encourage and comfort, and will speak directly
to the heart. They will also be in agreement with the
revealed word of God. Ultimately it is the pastor who will
authenticate them publicly.

I have found on rare occasions, when the word spoken

has a human or demonic origin, that there is a sensation of being hit by something very negative, like a cold feeling in the stomach. From the front it is observable that the heads of the congregation bend very low or are clutched between the hands, as if everyone is waiting for the storm to blow out. The intended prophecy is judged without even a word being spoken by the pastor.

Handling 'repentance' prophecies

There is nothing like a loud, unloving call to repentance to unsettle a congregation. If this goes unchecked, it can be the death knell to establishing a prophetic ministry as a normal part of a church's life. Often the very sincere people are taken in by it and become very agitated as they seek to make an appropriate response, and the others simply ignore it.

Such prophecies usually come in one of two ways. There is the obvious saying, 'God says you must repent. If you don't he will come with severe judgement.' Then there is a much subtler form, which goes something like this: 'My children, I desire to pour out my Spirit upon you, but you will need to soften your hard hearts.'

Where there is a biblical call to repentance, it usually has three ingredients. This is illustrated in Revelation in the letters of the risen Christ to the seven churches in Asia Minor. First, the call is corporate, to the whole congregation. Second, it starts with an affirmation concerning the good things that Jesus sees in their life together. Third, when the call to repentance comes it is always specific. For the church at Ephesus (Revelation 2:4) it is their 'lack of love'; for Pergamum (2:14) it is their 'false teaching'; for Thyatira it is their 'sexual immorality'; for Sardis (3:1) it is their 'spiritual deadness'.

As a rule, repentance-type prophecies should not be allowed in the context of public worship. Instead they should be written out and submitted to the pastor and the leadership team. This should be made clear to the congregation when the pastor lays down the structures for the practical operation of the prophetic gift.

It is necessary actively to cultivate and mature this ministry in the ongoing life of a congregation. It would seem that in the Old Testament many prophets operated within 'schools of prophets', and in the New Testament most of the prophets also operated in groups. As this ministry is established in a local church, it is important that those with the particular prophetic gifting are gathered together so that, in a 'school', their giftings can be affirmed and matured.

School for prophets

The first school I started came about as the direct result of a prophetic word. At a youth conference a teenager told me that whenever he looked at me God seemed to be saying the same thing to him. The word was that I should start a fellowship for young leaders and a school for prophets.

Over a number of years, as I sought scriptural insight for this project, I discovered to my surprise that in the Bible there regularly seemed to be a group of prophetic people who gathered around an authoritative prophetic figure. They were known as the company of the prophets or the disciples of a particular prophet. Isaiah gave these instructions: 'Bind up the testimony and seal up the law among my disciples' (Isaiah 8:16).

When Samuel anointed Saul as king of Israel, he gave him a number of signs to authenticate what he had spoken to him regarding his kingship. One of these signs was that on his journey home he would pass through Gibeah, where there was a Philistine garrison (see 1 Samuel 10:5). Here he would meet a procession of prophets who were returning from a worship celebration. Another part of the sign was that when he met them the Spirit of God would come upon him in power and he too would prophesy. It would seem from the context that these prophets were in fellowship with each other and probably ministered together at similar gatherings of worship.

In the days of Elijah and Elisha, the school concept is slightly more developed. Elijah had a revelation that the Lord was about to take him to heaven. This would happen in the vicinity of the River Jordan (see 2 Kings 2:1ff). Elisha accompanied Elijah as they made their way to the Jordan, and at Bethel and Jericho they were met by a company of prophets who had received a revelation that Elijah was about to be taken by the Lord. On each occasion they asked Elisha whether he was aware that the Lord was about to take Elijah, and both times he replied in the affirmative. When Elijah and Elisha arrived at the Jordan, 50 men of the company of the prophets met them, probably from Jericho. The number is significant and probably represents the maximum number for such a school.

In this incident we are confronted with the fact that the prophets only had a partial revelation concerning the evolving situation. They knew that Elijah was going, but they did not see the finality of it. They had the revelation, but not the complete interpretation.

There was a similar situation with Agabus and Paul, recorded by Luke in the book of Acts. On one occasion the prophet Agabus took Paul's belt and tied his own hands and feet with it, then announced, 'The Holy Spirit says, "In this way the Jews of Jerusalem will bind the owner of this belt and will hand him over to the Gentiles"' (Acts 21:11).

Paul was certainly taken into custody by the Gentiles, but the Jews did not hand him over.

On the Jordan's banks, Elisha took his cloak, rolled it up and struck the water. Miraculously the river divided, and the two prophets crossed over together. On the far bank Elijah asked Elisha if there was anything he could do for him before he went, and Elisha requested a 'double portion' of his spirit. In reply Elijah gave him a sign: if he saw Elijah being taken, then his request would be granted.

Suddenly a chariot and horses appeared, surrounded by fire, and Elisha saw his friend and mentor disappear in a whirlwind. He then picked up Elijah's cloak and struck the river, asking for the God of Elijah to intervene on his behalf. Again miraculously the waters divided, and Elisha crossed back over.

The school of prophets watched this unfolding and recognized through the divided river that Elisha's request had been granted. As a group, however, they wanted to go to look for Elijah, because it was not an uncommon occurrence for the Spirit of God to pick him up and place him in a different location. This was a problem that had confronted Obadiah, who was in charge of Ahab's palace. Obadiah was afraid that if he told his master that he had met Elijah and that he intended to visit him, the prophet would suddenly disappear. 'I don't know where the Spirit of the Lord may carry you when I leave you,' he said (1 Kings 18:12).

Elisha told the school of prophets not to seek Elijah, but they persisted and searched the surrounding countryside for three days, without success. When they returned, Elisha castigated them.

From the narrative in the second book of Kings, it would seem that Elisha had a close and developing relationship with the school of prophets. During a time of national famine they met with him (see 2 Kings 4:4), and they came to Elisha with their accommodation problems. The place where they met with Elisha was too small and they suggested to the prophet that they should all go to the forest near the Jordan and collect timber for a new building. The prophet agreed and went with them.

I often wondered how the school functioned prophetically, and a certain situation gave me some insight into this question. John Wimber was invited by a number of London churches to lead a conference based at Wembley. In the days leading up to the conference I was praying for John and these words came clearly into my mind: 'The Lord announced the word, and great was the company of those who proclaimed it.' I looked up this quote in a concordance and found that it was Psalm 68:11.

On the eve of the conference I telephoned John in his hotel room. I told him that I had been praying for him and that the Lord had seemed to give me a scripture for him. We discussed it at length. John said that the word the Lord had given him was simply that he wanted his church to minister in the power of the Holy Spirit. As he shared this, I suddenly saw that John had the revelation and three thousand leaders were going to hear the word. It was the Lord's intention that they should take this and make it happen within the churches and groups for which they were responsible.

I saw that it did not really matter who actually received the revelation. If the school 'weighed' it and thought it was from the Lord, that was enough. They could all then take it with authority to the people. This raises the question of whether the great prophets who functioned with schools always heard the Lord themselves, or were just speaking what the school had received. I think the latter could in some cases be true.

There are many ways in which schools could meet profitably. The first would be as an expression of the local church, which could be extended to a gathering of the prophetic people from churches in the general area. There could also be city-wide schools, as well as a national one.

I have found the following to be a helpful format for the gathering of the school for a day or evening together. We divide our time into two halves, the first given to worship and teaching, the second to listening and sharing.

During the second period I find that the word usually comes in one of two ways. It may be spontaneous and spoken from the floor as the recipient receives it, and this is obviously of benefit. Or I find that the words with the most impact are those that are brought along to the gathering, having been received beforehand.

Often prophets have received such words over a period of time, in dreams and visions or as they wait on the Lord in prayer. The following is an example from the nationwide school, which gathered at St Andrew's, Chorleywood, for two years. This word was given in September 1999 and came from a senior leader in the church.

The word concerned our relationship with money. The prophet believed the Lord had shown him that we were a nation who worshipped money and that this had replaced the Lord in the affections of the people. He expanded this word from revelations that he had received. He said that for the church to be able to speak into the situation with conviction, we needed to obey the Lord as regards our money – meaning that each believer would give a basic tenth of their salary to the Lord's work, as well as being generous with all that they had.

After this word was given, we waited on the Lord. Two or three others came and shared a similar word, which they had been given prior to the meeting. There were 220 people at the gathering, many of whom would be preaching in their own churches the following weekend. The Lord had given the word and great was the company of the preachers. I know one congregation that, after this word was given, pledged an extra £20,000 to the Lord's work. This amount came from those people who had not formerly given to the Lord the money due to him.

Taking action on prophetic words

At times I have been leading a meeting when I have heard the prophets say words such as, 'The power of God is present to heal the sick,' or, 'God is pouring out his love into people's hearts.' On such occasions I will stop the worship and ask people to stand quietly in the presence of God. Often revelation will come concerning physical conditions which the Lord is beginning to heal. At other times I have just encouraged people to welcome the Holy Spirit, who at that moment is seeking to pour the love of God into their hearts.

It is important that significant prophecies are brought before the church leadership and discussed by them. At St Andrew's we did this under the title 'What is the Spirit saying to the church?' Many initiatives concerning the work among youth and the planting of new congregations have come out of the prophetic word. Such referral gives the leadership the opportunity to view the present prophetic word against what they already believe the Lord has revealed concerning the life and direction of the church.

Members of the congregation will at times receive dreams, prophecies, pictures and words from the inspiration of the Holy Spirit. It is helpful to have two boxes in the church, one for 'prayer requests' and the other for 'visions'. In this way, people can write down what they believe God has spoken to them and put it in the box. It is helpful if they write their name and the date, with a short précis of the vision, dream or word and a note on what they think it means. Again, where significant revelation comes, it is important that the leadership should see it and, where appropriate, see how it can be incorporated into the church's life. Prophetic revelation always leads to prayer.

8

Music, Worship and the Prophetic

They sang a new song. (Revelation 5:9)

God has woven music and singing throughout his creation.
In the Psalms we read that the stars, the valleys, the mountains, the birds, the heavens and the hills sing. In
Zephaniah 3:17 we see the wonderful truth that God himself sings over us. Music flows out from the very heart of
God the Father. Music can be used to bless or destroy, but
most importantly it can be used as a vehicle to glorify, honour and worship the living God. God inhabits the praises
of his people. His presence is ushered in by Spirit-breathed
music. Hearts are inspired to worship God, and within this
context of worship and instrumental music, prophetic
utterance is often released.

The key to the release of prophetic worship is the relationship between the worship leader and the leader of the
singers and musicians. The worship leader is the person
who is overseeing the worship. This would normally be
the pastor, who would have the ultimate authority during
the act of worship.

The leader of the singers and musicians, although under
the pastor's authority, is also a co-leader with the pastor.

The best example I can give for this comes from my rugby-playing days. When we lived in Cornwall I played senior rugby for Camborne. I played at fly half and developed a very close playing relationship with my scrum half. We often said of each other, 'He always knew where I would be and I always knew what he would do.' This is the goal of the pastor and the leader of the musicians and singers as they both seek to be in touch with the leading of the Holy Spirit.

As we go on to study this theme, we will find that such a mutual sensitivity to the leading of the Holy Spirit is at the very heart of prophetic worship.

Prophetic worship in response to God's intervention

For the Hebrews, music was part of the fabric of their everyday lives. Within their vibrant culture, social and religious events were accompanied by singing, music and dancing. The whole range of human emotions, from joy to sorrow, was interpreted through music and song. They also expressed their hearts to God in worship.

Our first example of prophetic worship is taken from Exodus. This story of the birth of a nation is a story of God's miraculous intervention. For 400 years his people had been living in Egypt, but latterly they had become slaves of Pharaoh, who had increased his demands on them until their lives had become impossible. At their lowest ebb, the people had started to cry out to the Lord in prayer, and he had replied by revealing himself to Moses in the fire of a burning bush. Moses was told to go to Pharaoh with the message that the Lord commanded him to release the Hebrews from slavery and allow them to worship the living God. It was God's intention from the very beginning that his people should be a worshipping community.

Pharaoh's initial reaction was one of indolence, and he refused to allow the people to leave. After a series of plagues, however, he relented and gave permission – only to retract it soon afterwards. This situation reached a crisis when the Lord sent the Angel of Death through the nation to kill the firstborn of all people and animals. The Lord protected his own people by telling them to put the blood of a lamb on the lintels of their homes. This was a sign to the Angel of Death that no one within the building was to be harmed by the judgement. After this night of terror, it is recorded that Pharaoh said to Moses and Aaron, 'Up! Leave my people, you and the Israelites! Go, worship the Lord as you have requested' (Exodus 12:31).

That very night the nation started to move out of Egypt. They found themselves being pursued by Pharaoh and his army. The terrified Israelites were caught between the Red Sea and the advancing Egyptian army, but Moses exhorted them to stand their ground because the Lord would deliver them and dispose of the Egyptians. He said to the people, 'The LORD will fight for you; you need only to be still' (14:14).

As the nation waited on the Lord, he sent a powerful east wind that made a path through the sea. It was along this path, flanked by walls of water, that the nation walked to freedom. Once they were through to the other side, the sea resumed its normal place and the Egyptian army was drowned.

As a response to this, Moses the prophet was inspired to write 'The Song of the Sea' (see Exodus 15). This song recalls all that the Lord had done on Israel's behalf and the way he had acted like a warrior who brought the nation victory. The Lord is exalted as the incomparable God, and Moses acknowledges him for the first time as king. This is a prophetic song, inspired by God's intervention in the life of a nation. The emerging prophetic worship leader will also respond to God in a similar way.

As I described in an earlier chapter, I met an elderly lady in the pouring rain outside my daughter's new flat, and she commented, 'The Lord is speaking and no one is listening.' I believe she was right in what she said, as rain is a scriptural symbol of both blessing and judgement. The prophets say that God sends both the former and the latter rains. These come first to soften the soil for sowing and then to water the growing seed. This is very different from the rains the Lord sent in the days of Noah.

The Sunday after I met that lady, I recalled her words in a sermon. I made the point that if we had ears to hear and eyes to see, we would see the hand of God's judgement in the abnormal rains that had been visiting our nation for nearly a year. In many parts of the country they had wreaked havoc as whole villages and towns were engulfed in the water. In some places the flooding of the same homes was repeated on two or three occasions. After the service, our worship leader Nick Herbert told me that as he heard me recall what the lady had said, his heart was suddenly filled with a song. Its theme was simply, 'The Lord is speaking and no one is listening.' This is a prophetic worship leader's response to an act of God.

Prophetic dance

Miriam, the sister of Moses and Aaron, was a prophetess. After Moses and the people had sung 'The Song of the Sea', Miriam also responded spontaneously to what the Lord had done. She started to lead a dance, accompanied by the other women, many of whom played tambourines as they worshipped the Lord (see Exodus 15:20ff).

The emerging prophetic dancer can be a vehicle for a powerful visitation of the Holy Spirit. On one occasion at the New Wine family conference, the delegates were worshipping the Lord in the main pavilion. Suddenly a young woman started to dance across the front of the pavilion just below the stage. As she did this, the whole building became heavy with the presence of the Lord. The Lord was responding to the worship offered in the dance.

Probably the most powerful dance is the sort that is spontaneous. Sometimes at St Andrew's we gave permission to certain young women in our congregation to dance whenever they felt the Holy Spirit was prompting them to do so. This often ushered in a visitation from the Spirit of God in powerful ways. I believe this is because dance can speak directly to our hearts in ways that words cannot.

In the case of Miriam, as she led the dance she was also inspired in song: 'Sing to the LORD, for he is highly exalted. The horse and its rider he has hurled into the sea' (Exodus 15:21). This was a prophetic exhortation to the people literally to sing to the Lord because of what they had experienced of his love and power. The intention of the prophetic exhortation was to inspire people's hearts and lead them to worship.

In the days of the Judges, Jabin the king of Canaan and Sisera his commander cruelly oppressed the Israelites (see Judges 4:1ff). To counteract this, the Lord raised up the prophetess Deborah and at the Lord's command she went with her commander Barak into battle against Jabin. Through the Lord's intervention, the victory for Deborah was secured. Again we have a Holy Spirit-inspired song which Deborah and Barak sang together (see Judges 5). This again was prophetic and was in response to the actions of God. Prophesying in song is to sing out words under the inspiration of the Holy Spirit. This may include words predicting the future, words of exhortation and words of praise.

Instruments and supernatural sounds

Instruments have a vital part to play in prophetic worship. We first encounter an example of this after the anointing of Saul by the prophet Samuel (see 1 Samuel 10:1ff). Having just anointed Saul and told him that he was going to be king of Israel, Samuel tells him about the major signs which would authenticate his message. The third of these was that Saul would go to Gibeah, where there was a Philistine outpost. As Saul approached the town he would meet 'a procession of prophets coming down from the high place with lyres, tambourines, flutes and harps being played before them, and they will be prophesying' (v. 5). The prophetic musicians were using a variety of stringed, wind and percussion instruments.

Here we are introduced to 'supernatural sounds'. The Holy Spirit can inspire prophetic musicians with musical sounds, which on occasion can actually become the vehicle of the word – although this will not necessarily be so. In this case, it was the sounds themselves that ushered in the presence of God.

Once I was able to spend three weeks with David Manse, the presenter of *100 Huntley Street*. This is a Christian television programme which is broadcast out of Toronto each weekday morning. During my stay David invited me to host a week of meetings, and this involved conducting a ten-minute interview each morning. Toronto was celebrating a special English week, so I invited onto the programme five people who had emigrated to Canada from the UK and become Christians in their new country.

While I was researching for the programme, I was introduced to a musician named Ruth Fazel. She was a violinist
and played for a national orchestra. I suggested that she
should bring her violin onto the show and play a short
piece of music during the interview. She agreed, but said
that she would like to play as the Holy Spirit directed her.
This was a very new idea to me, and I must admit that I
did wonder what sort of music she would play!

The programme is transmitted live on television and is
performed in front of a packed studio auditorium. Before
she played, Ruth indicated that she would like to offer the
piece as an act of worship to God. As she played, the
sounds were electric. The audience seemed transfixed in
their seats. The presence of God was known from the
sounds of heaven, which Ruth was bringing to us
through the strings of her violin. I subsequently invited her
to the New Wine conference, and in a packed evening
meeting she again brought the presence of God into our
midst.

In 2 Kings we read about a coalition of three kings who
had joined together to fight the king of Moab (see chapter
3). This triumvirate comprised Joram, king of Israel,
Jehoshaphat, king of Judah, and the king of Edom. The
plan was that they should attack Moab from the south, but
after a seven-day march they discovered that there was no
water for either the soldiers or the animals (3:9).

The king of Israel became very depressed, blaming God
for their predicament, but Jehoshaphat asked whether
there was a prophet in the camp so that they could enquire
of the Lord through him. An officer reported that Elisha
was with them and this pleased Jehoshaphat, who knew
that the word of the Lord was with him.

When Elisha was summoned, he was rather contemptu-
ous of Joram and indicated that if it were not for

Jehoshaphat, he would have refused to be involved. He saw that two of the leaders were incompatible: Joram was the son of Ahab and Jezebel, two of the most wicked rulers of Israel, and in Samaria he worshipped the golden calves that Jeroboam had installed, putting himself in direct contact with destructive occult powers. In contrast, it is recorded that Jehoshaphat was a godly man who sought the will of God.

When such types of opposing powers are involved, there will often be a spiritual blockage preventing the voice of God from being heard. Elisha recognized this and knew that the oppressive powers of darkness had to be lifted. He therefore called upon a harpist to play. The narrative then records, 'While the harpist was playing, the hand of the LORD came upon Elisha' (3:15). This is another way of saying that the power of the Spirit of the Lord came upon the prophet as the 'supernatural sounds' were being played. The music brought a breakthrough, clearing the channels for God to speak.

Enveloped by musical sounds, Elisha started to see the Lord's intentions regarding the situation. He saw that the Lord would provide water in the desert in a most unlikely way. The people were to dig ditches across the valley, which the Lord would fill with water without the intervention of rain. They would then defeat the Moabites and cause devastation in the major cities, the forests and the wells.

Not only does the sound of the harp become a vehicle for prophecy, but it is also used by God to subdue and expel demonic forces. There was one occasion when, because of Saul's rebellion, the Spirit of the Lord departed from him and was replaced by an evil spirit that tormented him (see 1 Samuel 16:14). Saul's courtiers suggested that what was needed was a worship leader whose playing would subdue the power of the evil spirit, and so David was summoned. The man who was the future king was also a prophetic composer and worship leader, as his many songs indicate. The narrative records, 'Whenever the spirit from God came upon Saul, David would take his harp and play. Then relief would come to Saul; he would feel better, and the evil spirit would leave him' (16:23).

Worship structure through families

Once David had come to power and taken over responsibility for the worship of the Lord, he put in place an authority structure. This is recorded in 1 Chronicles 25. David did not appoint worship leaders by himself, but also involved the commanders of the army (v. 1). David saw the act of worship as a battle – not a physical but a spiritual one. It would seem that there were some organizational skills possessed by army commanders that had relevance to organizing the worship of God. The authority and structure of the worship was of the utmost importance.

David set apart musicians who played lyres, harps and cymbals. As they played their instruments, they were also to prophesy. The musicians involved were the sons of three men, under whose authority they ministered. The men were Asaph, Jeduthun and Heman, who was also one of the prophets who counselled King David. The three family leaders in turn were under the direct authority of the king. Under this general umbrella of authority were 288 relatives who were trained and skilled in music for the Lord.

These men and their families were set apart for the ministry of prophetic worship, which would have as its objective the thanking and praising of God. Although such worship was dependent upon the inspiration of the Holy Spirit, which by definition created freedom, there was also a very strong accountability structure.

The apostle Paul alludes to some of the same musical instruments in his letter to the church in Corinth. He refers to a noisy gong and clanging cymbals (1 Corinthians 13:1), and to the flute, harp and trumpet (14:7–8).

We can see God's prototype for prophetic worship in the situation after Solomon had completed the Temple. Once the Temple was finished, Solomon had the ark brought up and placed in the Holy of Holies. This was accompanied by an act of celebration involving the prophetic families of Asaph, Jeduthun and Heman (see 2 Chronicles 5:2ff). As the musicians played, 120 priests sounding trumpets accompanied them. Then the act of worship moved towards a crescendo: 'The trumpeters and singers joined in unison, as with one voice, to give praise and thanks to the LORD. Accompanied by trumpets, cymbals and other instruments, they raised their voices in praise to the LORD' (5:13).

The prophetic utterance that verbalized the worship was simply this: 'He is good; his love endures for ever' (5:13). This stanza is taken from a song which David wrote to celebrate the taking of the ark to Jerusalem from the house of Obed-Edom. The ark had been there for eight years as a result of Uzzah a non-Levite touching it. These words were also sung at the rebuilding of the Temple after the exile (see Ezra 3:11), and when Jeremiah prophesied restoration after the exile (see Jeremiah 33:11). It is a prime example of how a prophetic utterance can be given in the past and then anointed once again for a present situation.

The emerging prophetic worship leader

Emerging prophetic worship leaders will above all be worshippers themselves, and will spend many hours alone with their instruments worshipping the Lord. It is in this quiet place that they will learn to hear the sounds of God, and it is here that words reflecting God's desires for his worshipping people will be received in the form of songs. Spending a good deal of time in solitude and quiet to hear God's voice is also important for those who would dance before the Lord.

From the place of solitude the leader will discern what the anointed songs are for that particular season of the Spirit. It seems that there are certain songs anointed in a church for a season, and outside that time the same anointing is not on them. At the consecration of the Temple, it became clear that the simple stanza from David's song was where the anointing of God rested. As the musicians played and the singers sang, it released a powerful presence of God into the situation.

Above all, what defines prophetic worship leaders is the anointing of the Holy Spirit. They learn to discern the Lord's presence and to know when he is speaking and bringing inspiration. This is very difficult to quantify, but such anointing is obvious when it is present.

In the 1970s I had my first encounter with such a worship leader when I met the Fisherfolk, a worship group from Houston, Texas, who had come to England with their pastor Graham Pulkingham. Their church had experienced a visitation of the Holy Spirit, which had filled the lives of the congregation in new ways and had released in many people the various gifts of the Holy Spirit. One of the main ways they were experiencing this new life was in worship.

The Fisherfolk had come to the UK to lead celebrations in many of the cathedrals as well as to conduct conferences for parish churches. After they had visited Chorleywood, I was invited to accompany them on a number of national tours and speak at their meetings. On one occasion we did a tour in the West Country and on the first night we came to a church that was packed, but the atmosphere was very dead. I sensed a certain opposition to what the Fisherfolk represented and talked this over with Mike Kennedy, who was the main worship leader. He said he had sensed it himself, but we were not to worry – a sense of freedom would start to come as they worshipped the Lord. He then invited me to stand up front with the band.

After a general welcome, the worship began. From the first note sounded on Mike's guitar, it seemed that the Spirit of God fell upon the worship band. It was as if they were in a circle of God's presence. As I was standing in the midst of this group, I too could sense this, although I was in no way leading the worship. Since those days, in many places, I have seen that the main feature of emerging prophetic worship leaders is that as soon as they start to lead worship they make a channel for the presence of God.

Since those way-off days, I have also seen that each new move of the Spirit brings with it new songs which express something of the new life of the Spirit.

The power of God in prophetic worship

In 2 Chronicles we read, 'The temple of the LORD was filled with a cloud, and the priests could not perform their service because of the cloud, for the glory of the LORD filled the temple of God' (5:13–14). This is the objective of prophetic worship. The worshippers are caught up in the presence of God. All such worship leads to silence and an encounter with God.

After the ark was placed in the Temple, Solomon prayed that God would use the building for his purposes. He asked that the building would be a place where God dwelled and where his name would be known. He asked that it would be a place where forgiveness and justice could be found. He realized that at times enemies would defeat God's people, and he asked that in the Temple they might be restored. Knowing that there would be times when God had to judge the nation, he asked that if repentance was made in the Temple, then God would forgive and reverse his decision. He asked that through prayer natural disasters would be averted. He requested that the sick would be healed and that foreigners would find mercy, that armies would be helped and that those taken captive would be released (see 2 Chronicles 6).

When Solomon had prayed in this way and had dedicated the Temple to the Lord, the fire of God fell upon the sacrificial offering he had made, and the glory of the Lord filled the Temple. As a result the worship leaders were unable to enter the building and those outside fell on their faces and worshipped, thanking God and saying, 'He is good; his love endures for ever' (7:3). There is a similar vision of heavenly worship in Revelation 5, when the 24 elders fall down before the Lamb and sing a 'new song' of worship.

Those who experience the presence of God today as the people did in the days of Solomon testify to the outworking of such worship in their communities. On one occasion I was speaking at a large Pentecostal church in Rotterdam, Holland. At the end of the meeting two Colombians came and wanted to talk about some of the things that I had been saying. They had a business in Holland and had just returned from a trip to Colombia to see their families. They told me how God was coming in great power to certain church buildings and stadiums over there. As the people gathered to worship, they told me, the power of God would fill the buildings where they were. When the believers left the buildings to go home, they would often stop on the street and continue to worship. The power of God was so present on the group that anyone who joined them on the street also dynamically experienced the presence of God.

9

The Prophet as the Healer

I am the Lord, who heals you. (Exodus 15:26)

Throughout the Scriptures God is revealed as the source of all healing. This healing is not confined to people's physical, spiritual or emotional condition, but rather involves every aspect of life where disease has entered in. The main ministers of this healing in the Bible were the prophets.

Bitter water becomes sweet

After the trauma of the Exodus, the prophet Moses led the people from the banks of the Red Sea to the Desert of Shur. This was a three-day march, during which they were unable to find any water. When they eventually came to a spring, the water in it was undrinkable. The people blamed Moses for their predicament and he in turn sought the Lord, who told him to throw a piece of wood into the water. As he did this, the bitter water became sweet and drinkable. This was the first time God showed his healing power to the people of the Exodus (see Exodus 15:22ff).

After this episode, the Lord made a promise to his people. If they listened to him and obeyed him, then he would not bring on them the diseases from which the Egyptians suffered. He said, 'I am the LORD, who heals you' (15:26) and the word used here for 'heal' means to mend by stitching. On another occasion the Lord said, 'Worship the LORD your God, and his blessing will be on your food and water. I will take away sickness from among you' (Exodus 23:25ff).

The first recorded miracle of the prophet Elisha also involved water. In Jericho there was an ancient well. The water in it had become contaminated and the land on which it was poured became unproductive. The men of the city came to Elisha and described the situation to him, and he instructed that a new bowl should be filled with salt and brought to him. As with Moses and the piece of wood, Elisha was being led by the Spirit of the Lord. In obedience he threw the salt into the spring, and as he did this the word of the Lord came to him: 'This is what the LORD says: "I have healed this water. Never again will it cause death or make the land unproductive"' (2 Kings 2:21).

Prophetic actions

The above example illustrates how prophets are used to bring healing to areas of the creation where disease has entered in. Often when prophets are involved in the physical healing of a person, the Lord asks them to perform an action first. In the case of Peter's mother-in-law, Jesus touched her hand and then the fever left her (see Matthew 8:15). With two blind men, Jesus touched their eyes before he spoke the prophetic word which resulted in healing (see 9:29). With another blind man, he made some mud with his saliva and put it on the man's eyes, then told him to go and wash in the Pool of Siloam (see John 9:6–7). He touched the leper before healing came (see Mark 1:41), and told a man with a crippled hand to stand up and stretch it out (see 3:5).

David Pytches, my colleague at St Andrew's for 17 years, tells of a time when he was ministering in Paris. A lady who had lost the sight of an eye came for prayer. David went through the normal procedure of finding out when it had happened and what events had given rise to the blindness. Normally he would have invited the Holy Spirit to come and would have ministered in Jesus' name as he felt the Lord was directing him. This time, however, to his astonishment, he heard the Lord say, 'Spit on her eye.' The community in which he was ministering was middle class and affluent, the lady in question was dressed very elegantly, and David describes how he struggled to be obedient to what he believed the Lord had said. Eventually he plucked up courage and asked her if she minded him spitting on her eye. She was somewhat perplexed, but agreed. As soon as he put spittle on the eye, the healing came. Her sight was fully restored.

On one occasion I was praying for a man who had a severe lower back condition that had all but crippled him, and affected every area of his life. I laid my hand on his lower back and asked Jesus to bring healing. After a few moments, when nothing particular seemed to be happening, I sensed I heard the Lord say, 'Tell him to touch his toes.' This seemed as irrational as it was cruel. This man could hardly stand upright, let alone bend over. However, I took my courage in both hands and suggested that in his own time he should try to touch his toes. As he did this, healing was released upon him.

In the prophetically inspired healings of the Old Testament, prophetic action very often played a major role. In 2 Kings, Naaman was an important army officer with a young Jewish girl serving in his home who had been captured in a campaign. Naaman had contracted leprosy and the little girl suggested that he should travel to Israel and visit the prophet Elisha, who would heal him. Naaman went with the permission of his own king and carried a letter with him to the king of Israel, instructing him to have Naaman cured. This sent shock waves through the palace. Elisha heard what had happened and asked that Naaman be sent directly to him.

When Naaman arrived at his door, he sent out a messenger to tell him, 'Go, wash yourself seven times in the Jordan, and your flesh will be restored and you will be cleansed' (5:10). The message and the fact that Elisha did not come out to greet him infuriated Naaman, and it took great persuasion by his servant to make him do what the prophet had said. As soon as he washed himself seven times in the river, however, his flesh was restored and became clean like that of a young boy.

Prophetic actions were also involved when Elijah and Elisha raised two dead boys back to life. On the first occasion, the son of the widow of Zarephath died and Elijah took the body and laid it on a bed. He then stretched himself out on the boy three times, each time crying, 'O LORD my God, let this boy's life return to him!' (1 Kings 17:21). On the third cry the boy's life returned. Elisha raised the dead son of the Shunammite woman in a similar way. After the prophetic actions were performed, the resurrection came (see 2 Kings 4:1ff).

In every situation in which emerging prophets find themselves ministering, they need to be aware that the Lord may want them to perform an action. After this action the word may come which will facilitate healing.

A model for healing

For over three decades I have been involved in the leadership of churches that have nurtured and encouraged the healing ministry. Initially we took as our model the teaching that James describes in his epistle. He teaches that if anyone is sick, he should initiate healing by inviting the leadership of the church to pray over him. The leadership should anoint the sick person with oil and pray for him in the name of the Lord. James indicates that if the leadership has faith, then the Lord will answer the prayer and healing will ensue. He also teaches that unconfessed sin could be a cause of the person's sickness, and therefore he encourages confession before anointing and prayer (see James 5:13ff). It seems that the God-given authority to minister healing was upon the office of leadership.

Once we as a church embarked on this, we soon discovered the mystery surrounding healing. Our experience was that some people were healed, but many were not and many died from terminal illnesses. There was one common denominator, however, and this was that everyone who was prayed with had an experience of God. This usually meant that the person concerned came to know God's peace and comfort. If the illness proved terminal, then they would have a hope which enabled them to face death without fear.

Seeing God's intentions for healing

In my search for the healing of others, I started to see that there was also another model. Paul describes this in his first letter to the church in Corinth. He anticipates that when the church gathers for worship, the gifts of the Spirit will be present in individual believers, including gifts of healing, miraculous powers, faith, and the ability to distinguish between spirits (see 1 Corinthians 12:7ff). I came to see, however, that the key to God operating in this way was revelation. If the prophet could see what God's intentions were, then he or she could minister healing with confidence.

There is an incident in John's Gospel that starts to cast a light on the place of the prophetic in healing. In Jerusalem there was a pool named Bethesda, and it was the gathering place for the sick people of the city. At certain times there was a manifestation of the power of God in the water, and those who managed to get into the pool at that time were healed (see John 5). Jesus walked through this large crowd of disabled people and stopped by one of the invalids. He learned from those around him that the man had been ill for 38 years. Jesus asked the man if he wanted to get well. The invalid did not recognize that Jesus had the power to heal him, and in reply said that he had no one to put him in the pool when the healing power came to the waters. Jesus said to him, 'Get up! Pick up your mat and walk' (5:8). At once the man was cured; he picked up his mat and walked.

This particular healing teaches us a number of important lessons. As he looked at the man, Jesus had a revelation concerning his Father's intention. In response to those who opposed what he had done, he said, 'The Son can do nothing by himself; he can do only what he sees his Father doing, because whatever the Father does the Son also does' (John 5:19). Jesus saw that, among this great crowd of sick and suffering people, his Father intended to heal just one person.

In my travels in India I have noticed that the entrances to the temples are strewn with cripples, people who are seriously ill, and many who are suffering from serious pain. This is how it would have been in Jerusalem when Peter and John were making their way to pray in the Temple as described in Acts. A man who had been crippled from birth accosted them, begging the two men for money. Peter replied, 'Look at us!' (Acts 3:4). Peter was looking to see whether there were any indications that the Father was going to work a miracle for him. As he looked, he saw God's intentions and said simply, 'In the name of Jesus Christ of Nazareth, walk' (v. 6).

Similarly, in Lystra there was a cripple who had been lame since birth. With many others he was listening to Paul preach about Jesus. We read, 'Paul looked directly at him, saw that he had faith to be healed and called out, "Stand up on your feet!" At that, the man jumped up and began to walk' (Acts 14:1ff).

A great question remains about God's care and concern for those in the crowd who were in a far worse condition than the man whom he healed. The emerging prophet will always have to live with this mystery. Such healings, which result from revelation, are signs of the kingdom of God and in the area in which they happen they cause wonder. If sincere people seek their meaning, they will find a living Jesus.

We saw in the life of the cripple at the pool of Bethesda that his physical condition was the direct result of moral and spiritual disobedience. As a result Jesus warned him not to return to the actions that had led to his illness. Again, on another occasion, when four men lowered a cripple through the roof and into the presence of Jesus, he said to the paralytic, 'Take heart, son; your sins are forgiven' (Matthew 9:2).

Prophets watch and listen to hear what the Father will say regarding the person to whom they seek to bring healing.

From the rational to revelation to healing

On one occasion I was speaking at a meeting in Northern Ireland. It was part of a week of meetings held at Rostrevor, the home of a Christian community led by Cecil and Myrtle Kerr, and people had come from many parts of the country.

I spoke at an evening meeting that started at seven and went on until nearly midnight. Just as I was about to leave, a woman approached me and asked me if I would pray with her husband. I asked why they had not come for prayer earlier, and she said that she had fallen on the floor under the power of the Holy Spirit. Lying there, she had heard the voice of Jesus telling her to go and fetch her husband Peter, who had been confined to a wheelchair for ten years and in continuous pain for fourteen. She had returned to Peter, who was being looked after in a hospice staffed by Catholic nuns, and had insisted that he got up and went with her to the meeting. When I asked her where her husband was now, she pointed to a slight figure curled up in a chair at the back of the building. I was feeling tired by then, and decided that I would pray over them together, simply asking God to give them his grace.

We walked towards her husband until, halfway down the hall, I heard Jesus say to me, 'I will raise him up.' Suddenly I felt an almost physical surge of faith rise within me, and I approached Peter saying quietly, 'Jesus will raise you up.' As I spoke these words, Peter slid to the floor and lay very still. I felt I could see a deep well of pain within him. Kneeling next to him, I placed my hand on his stomach, saying, 'I break the power of pain in Jesus' name.' I had hardly spoken the words when he began to sob deeply and become agitated. After about 20 minutes, during which he was clearly in great emotional pain, the agitation left him and he became still and quiet. I heard him whispering and thought I heard him praying. Finally, I suggested to his wife that she should leave Peter on the floor until he indicated that he wanted to go, and I made my way to bed.

The next morning my thoughts were entirely on the talk that I was to give at half past ten, and the events of the previous night had been pushed out of my mind. I arrived at the meeting and sat with my eyes closed during the opening time of worship. Suddenly I was conscious of someone tugging on the sleeve of my sweater – probably Cecil Kerr, I thought. It was nearly time for me to speak. I opened my eyes, and was absolutely amazed to see Peter standing in front of me. 'I'm completely healed!' he said, with his arms outstretched towards me. We embraced and wept together, then I invited him and his wife to tell the gathering what had happened to them.

They explained that shortly after I had left the meeting, Peter had been taken home by his wife and put to bed in the normal way. On waking, Peter had felt a power like fire flowing through his body from his head to his feet. As he lay there, he started to flex his arms and legs and, to his joy and amazement, he realized that he had been healed. He rose from his bed, took a shower, dressed himself and then went to collect his wife. Together they had walked a mile to be at the meeting.

Peter said that the key moment for him was when I had said over him, 'I break the power of pain in Jesus' name.' He then told a most heartbreaking story. When he was a small child, his parents had taken his sister and emigrated to America, placing him in an orphanage. Now aged 57, he had never had any contact with his family since that time. From the orphanage he had been put in a series of homes, where those with a responsibility to care for him had physically and sexually abused him. As I had spoken the words of release over him, he had felt as if he was vomiting out the pain of a lifetime.

This is an example of how the emerging prophet will go from the rational through revelation and on to healing. When Peter's wife told me about the situation, my first response was one of compassion. It was a rational response. I imagined how traumatic it must be to have the partner you love confined to a wheelchair. I thought of her pain and sadness. I decided that I would pray for them together. I would ask the Lord to lift from her the weight of the previous ten years and refresh her in every area through the power of the Holy Spirit. For Peter I would ask the Lord to give him all the resources he would need to be able to deal with his pain and confined situation.

It is so easy to confine the situation just to the rational and not look for a miraculous intervention from God. Although it does not relate to healing, there is an occasion in the Bible that illustrates this principle very well. David, the Israelite king, had completed his palace and was discussing the building of a Temple with the prophet Nathan. The king was saying to Nathan that he had a palace of cedar, whereas the ark of the covenant was housed in a tent. Nathan advised the king to build the Temple because God was with him (see 1 Chronicles 17:1ff). In the prophet's rational mind, this was the next thing to be done. That night, however, Nathan had a revelation to the effect that it was not the Lord's intention that David should build the Temple.

As I walked down the hall towards Peter, my firm intention was to ask God's grace to enable him to cope in the situation. I could not take my eyes off the little, emaciated figure. Then came the revelation when I heard the Lord say, 'I will raise him up.' With the coming of revelation the gift of faith comes into play, and the prophet is full of the knowledge that without a shadow of doubt God is going to do what he has said. In the case of Peter, we did not get off to a great start because when I spoke the words 'Jesus will raise you up', he fell off the chair and collapsed onto the floor. I still knew that the healing was coming, however.

In these situations there is always a key that will unlock the healing. Peter was lying on the floor in a foetal position. I knelt next to him and watched. After a few minutes, I saw within his stomach area a pool of pain. The breaking of the pain removed the barrier to healing. That was the key.

Stages of healing

Sometimes in a healing situation, the revelation will come in two or three stages. This means that initially the person receives a partial healing. In the New Testament, when Jesus ministered to the blind man, he spat on the man's eyes and as a result the man saw people as if they were walking trees. Then Jesus put his hands on the man's eyes, and that time he saw clearly.

Once I was with a team and we were praying for the sick. One young woman had very severe arthritis; her hands and arms were bound with leather supports and she shuffled when she walked. Two people were praying for her, and I was standing behind watching.

A revelation came to one of those praying, and they prayed according to what they had been shown. Suddenly the power of God started to come to the upper part of the young woman's body. Her hands and arms experienced the heat of the Spirit. She asked that the leather supports be taken off, and started to move her hands freely. From the waist up she was completely healed.

Standing behind her, I could see her puffed-up knees and ankles, and I thought how wonderful it would be when the Spirit of the Lord flowed into that part of her body too. Sadly, however, I waited in vain and eventually she shuffled out of the meeting with her husband. They were both excited with what had happened, and later that evening she telephoned me to say that she was holding her baby after having washed her hair for the first time. She asked why the healing had stopped at her waist, but I had no answers.

A month later I was praying for her when I sensed that the Lord wanted me to visit her again and that he now intended to complete the healing. Mary and I drove to the young woman's home. We suggested that she should sit on a chair while we prayed for her. As Mary and I waited on the Lord, the revelation came and I heard the Lord say, 'It's to do with a childhood trauma.'

We stopped praying, and I asked her if that was so. She thought for some time and then said that there had been nothing significant that she could remember. We continued to pray, and again the Lord repeated the word. Eventually she shared an incident which had been deeply suppressed and of which she had been in total denial.

When she was eleven years old, she had come home from school one day and stood outside the kitchen where there was a terrible row in progress. She heard her mother shouting at her grandmother. Her father had left the family for another woman and her mother had subsequently entered into a new relationship. The row centred on who was going to bring up the girl. Her mother thought that the grandmother should accept the responsibility so that she could begin a new life. The girl opened the kitchen door to see her mother and grandmother lying on the floor.

Her mother was trying to choke her grandmother. The girl ran terrified from the room.

Having received the revelation in prayer, we put the cross of Jesus between the young woman and every way in which this event had impacted her life. At this point the healing power of God was released into her waist, knees and ankles, and within a very short while all the swelling had gone and her body had returned to normal. She subsequently became an active member of a dance group.

Discernment for healing

There will be times when emerging prophets encounter conditions in people where they will need to discern whether they are emotional, physical or demonic. Jesus met people who 'were ill with various diseases, those suffering severe pain, the demon-possessed, those having seizures, and the paralysed' (Matthew 4:24). Emerging prophets will start to have similar revelations.

Jesus discerned when abnormal behaviour was due to the presence of evil or unclean spirits inhabiting a person. There was the young boy in Luke's Gospel who would suddenly scream and go into convulsions while foaming at the mouth (see Luke 9:37ff). The force that overpowered him would try to kill him by throwing him into fire or water. There are many similar instances in the Gospels. Jesus also discerned that a woman who had been physically crippled for 18 years had in fact been crippled by the presence of a demon.

A young man who was deeply troubled came to see me. For many years he had been part of what he described as the 'party culture'. He had been heavily involved with the drug scene and, while under the influence, had seen many entities which he described as demons. Although married, he had adopted a sexually permissive lifestyle and went regularly for massage from a practising witch. When his first child was born, he had it taken to an altar in the forest and dedicated to the devil. While all this was taking place, the young man had been befriended by some Christians who spoke to him about the way of Christ. He eventually came to see the foolishness of his ways, but just believing in Jesus had not dealt with the torment and deep anger with which he struggled daily.

This was a blatant case of demonization. Once I started to pray for him, I sensed the presence of a personal evil. Through revelation I started to see the doors through which this uncleanness had entered. The way out for him was to confess the evil of the things he had welcomed into his life through those various doors, and then to renounce the hold that these powers had over him. After he had done this, I simply commanded that all evil leave him in the name of Jesus. At that point his face began to contort and he began to vomit and foam at the mouth as the spirit of Jesus drove evil from him. When all of this had gone, I encouraged him to welcome the Holy Spirit to fill his life and heart.

There will be other occasions when the emerging prophet will experience an almost identical situation. The person will feel confused and in torment, perhaps with physical manifestations such as shaking or crying out loud. In this case, however, the cause is to do with trauma and suppressed pain rather than a demonic presence.

In Chapter 2 I referred to a lady who had lost her young son seven years previously and had hidden away every sign of him in her house. Daily she was traumatized by the way in which he had died. They had been walking together when he had bent down to pick up something on the road. He had been struck by a lorry and killed instantly. She had been holding his hand when this happened. At our first meeting she had all the signs of being troubled by evil spirits, but the reason was actually her unresolved trauma. Eventually she asked me to pray with her, and when I did this I broke the power of pain in Jesus' name. This released a bout of screaming that must have lasted for 20 minutes. It sounded as if a demon had gone out from her, but it was simply the release of the suppressed trauma. As she had talked with me, I had received the revelation showing me that the key to her healing would be the release of trauma.

These are the fields through which emerging prophets will find themselves walking. In every case it is imperative that we seek the Lord for revelation concerning the person or situation to which we are ministering.

Sometimes I have been asked to pray with the leadership of a church, which may involve eight or ten people. As I have moved from one person to another, I have sometimes had a steady flow of revelation concerning their lives and God's calling on them. On other occasions, however, I have had nothing. This is equally true when it comes to praying for the sick. When I have no revelation, I simply welcome the Holy Spirit and invite the Lord to minister his life to the person for whom I am praying.

10

The Artist as the Prophet

I have filled him with the Spirit of God, with skill, ability
and knowledge in all kinds of crafts. (Exodus 31:3)

There have been many occasions when I have experienced
God in profound and unexpected ways. One such time
was when I first saw Holman Hunt's painting *The Light of
the World* based on the words of Jesus from the book of
Revelation. In the Bible narrative he is challenging the
church at Laodicea over their spiritual deadness. When I
first saw Hunt's picture, I was not a Christian and knew
nothing of its meaning, but it stirred something within my
spirit. Hunt's painting is revelatory. He depicts a risen
Jesus who is light in the surrounding darkness. He is humble and sensitive and stands waiting for an answer to his
knocking at a closed door. The door handle is missing:
only the person inside the house can open the door to him.
The painting is full of powerful imagery and prophetic
symbols.

Paintings have frequently had a powerful effect on me.
When I visited Rembrandt's house in Amsterdam, for
example, I found myself alone in a downstairs room. On
one wall were three etchings the artist had done which

depicted the death of Jesus. In the first the emphasis seemed to be on the crowd who were watching the grisly scene. The second highlighted the two thieves, while in the third the light fell upon Jesus. Everything else was subservient to this. The artist as prophet was taking the watcher through various aspects of the death of Jesus, finishing by highlighting the central truth, which was Jesus himself and his death on the cross.

For many years I have viewed the exhibits for the Turner Prize at the Tate Gallery and have also spent time in the Tate Modern and its equivalent in Amsterdam. Contemporary art in all its forms has always fascinated me. These exhibitions have mainly reflected the hopelessness and despair of our culture. One might say that up until now it is the secular artists who have been the prophets to our culture. They have interpreted the tormented and confused spirit of an age which on the whole has rejected God.

Now, however, prophets are starting to emerge within the churches. Through visions, dreams and the whispered word, God is speaking and the prophets are reflecting that in their utterances. In a similar way God is also raising up prophetic artists and revealing his word to them. These men and women have the greatest exposure of all. Millions in secular galleries and exhibitions will see the messages that God will speak through them. They will become one of the most powerful means of communicating truths about God in the coming days.

A seeing people

Often a prophecy can be a picture received by a member of the congregation, described and spoken out audibly. The prophetic artist works on the same principle, but where prophetic utterances deal with words and hearing, prophetic pictures deal with images and seeing. Also, while prophetic words are intended for the edification of God's people within the confines of the church building, prophetic images are intended for the world outside the church walls.

This is because visual prophetic images are less overtly Christian and so are more likely to be received by a person than prophetic words, especially if that person has certain prejudices against Christianity. Images can bypass the barriers put up by people who have preconceptions of what Christianity is about. Art has a way of getting round people's intellectual and emotional prejudices, because it always speaks indirectly – whether it is delivering a new message or asking a new question. Because of this subtlety and indirectness, art has a way of getting to the heart of the matter, where it is capable of moving even the most immovable men and women.

From ancient times, image-making has been part of the human consciousness. It is a primal instinct evident in the most ancient cave paintings. Primal man needed to understand the world around him, just as we do today. In the same way, pictures can give us answers to the needs within – not only physical needs, but also emotional and spiritual ones. Pictures act as maps to help us on the journey of life.

Many people in the world today are lost, and are looking for some meaningful symbols to give them guidance and direction. When they reach a crossroads in their life, they look around them for some sort of sign, and this is where prophetic artists come in. They are used by God to bring a message of hope, warning, encouragement or conviction.

People are looking for real answers to the problems they face. Could this be why so many people flock to an art gallery? The Tate Modern has become the most frequented museum in the world, and we must ask why all those people go there week after week. I believe that they are looking for something, seeking to be taken out of the mundane existence of everyday life, trying to glean some message of hope or direction for their lives.

The miracle of images is that they can change people's hearts. In the presence of a beautiful image, viewers take a step aside, losing their place as centre of their world. Beauty takes people's eyes away from their own problems and alerts them to a wider context, promoting selflessness.

Recently I saw an exhibition of Botticelli's illustrations to Dante's *Inferno* at the Royal Academy of Art. Held in the midst of the foot and mouth epidemic that devastated Britain's countryside, the anguish of the lost souls in Botticelli's drawings echoed the very real horror and despair of many farmers. On the morning I saw the exhibition I had read an article about the growing suicide rate in the farming community, and a specific case had been cited where a father of two had hanged himself the night before. The knowledge I had received in my mind filtered through to my heart as I gazed at Botticelli's extraordinary drawing of souls drowning in the abyss of pain and hopelessness, and I began to weep. I completely forgot about my own problems and began to see the situation the way God saw it, glimpsing a little of his compassion for a suffering community.

What is important here is that it was the beauty and exquisite skill of Botticelli's hand that sparked this reaction in me. The beauty of the picture spoke to my heart, while the newspaper article could only speak to my head. The other important thing to note is that it prompted me to pray for the farmers. In other words, not only did beauty prompt a heart response, but it also stirred my will into action. This is a universal truth. I believe that beauty by its very nature propels a person to act against injustice and fight for goodness.

Art can penetrate our emotional prejudices by showing us who we really are, by accurately reflecting our own pretensions, foibles and anxieties. When we look at a piece of art, we are holding up a mirror to our heart. The deep and hidden things in the dark closets of our heart are illuminated. Art sheds light into these dark corners of the soul, and shows us things we never knew were there.

The realization of what is in one's heart is the first step to healing, just as an alcoholic's confession of the addiction is the first step to recovery. Art is capable of bringing us into these honest confrontations with ourselves in an indirect rather than a confrontational way. This is why real art, although at first it may be a welcome escape from reality, will inevitably lead us into a face-to-face encounter with reality – but always in a different light from which it was originally seen.

In reflecting our own heart back to ourselves, art has the ability to remind us of dreams, hopes and desires we once had. In this way it acts as a memory trigger. Jesus came to heal the broken-hearted, to set the oppressed free and to release the prisoners. Prophetic artists are called to take on this ministry. For many people, the search for truth takes them down the wrong path, and they end up ensnared by the enemy who robs them of their freedom and ultimately of their life. Yet they do not know the one who can save them. Art encourages people to cry out by revealing a solution and a way out.

A work of art has the ability to rekindle forgotten dreams and hopes, and so lift people's eyes from the gutter and focus their gaze on the source of all hope and comfort, God himself. It is about stirring hearts to recognize what it is they were looking for the whole time – security, meaning, purpose, love, acceptance and peace. And these things are found in God alone.

The problem is that people have forgotten how to see. Their eyes have grown dim from despair. They have lost the hope that God can save them. In fact, they probably do not acknowledge that God exists at all. This is what Paul talks about in his letter to the Corinthians. There is a veil over people's hearts and minds that prevents them from seeing God. Unbelievers are trapped in their own blindness, in the circle of their own humanity.

Jesus' healing of the man born blind therefore has significance for all people, for 'nobody has ever heard of opening the eyes of a man born blind' (John 9:32). God is seeking to lift the scales from unbelievers' eyes by raising up artists to teach people how to see. This starts with the world around us. Everything created points back to a God who is the source of all things. The seen world points to an unseen, spiritual world. It is as if every object and being has its own soul, pointing us back to the Creator God.

Art deals with the human condition. It seeks to give an expression to human nature, our problems and experiences, in an effort to discover our place in history and in the universe and to throw light on our suffering and our joy. The ultimate incarnation was God becoming man in the person of Jesus Christ. He was not God as Spirit inhabiting a human body – the Holy Spirit was to do this on the day of Pentecost. Instead, he was fully God and fully human. His humanity cannot be overstated. He experienced the same range of human emotions as we do – pain, joy, disappointment, hunger, rejection from friends, loneliness, fear, abandonment.

We need to be honest about these very real emotions unless we, in seeking a disembodied purity and spirituality, should forget the humanity we are called to live out fully. God has called us to live in the natural as well as the spiritual realm. He has called us to redeem humanity and creation, to set our hands to work, to restore meaning in a society that is plagued with meaninglessness, futility and despair. The calling of the prophetic artist is to provide contemporary versions of the age-old answer of Christianity to the ways in which humanity's age-old questions are being asked both emotionally and intellectually today. The prophetic artist deals with a timely message specific to the age in which it is made, using the cultural tools of that age, and seeking to answer the questions asked by that age.

The role of the prophetic artist in society

Through the centuries artists have influenced the way we see the world. Images affect our understanding of outside reality, so a beautiful sunset is 'like a painting' and a beautiful landscape is 'picturesque'. An exciting possibility lies in wait for the prophetic artist to have an influence on how society sees the world, pointing to the truth of God's existence and the nature of his character. The prophetic artist is called to restore God to his place at the centre of all things.

As a culture, we have lost the ability to read the signs. We are guilty of Jesus' charge to the Pharisees and Sadducees: 'You know how to interpret the appearance of the sky, but you cannot interpret the signs of the times' (Matthew 16:3). Some other cultures still retain this sense. The case of Joanne Lees' boyfriend Peter Falconio going missing in Australia involves a people group who are still in touch with 'the signs of the times'. Aborigines were enlisted to help track down the whereabouts of Falconio's kidnapper by studying footprints – they are able to tell the size and type of being that made the prints, the direction travelled and even the time the imprint was made. As a people group, the Aborigines have developed a wide range of sensitivity to sight, smell and sound. This sensitivity is unknown in our Western culture, where our experience of outside reality has become so fused with technology that we have lost all groundedness in the places we inhabit and are unable to gauge what nature is telling us.

Timothy exhorts us to fix our eyes on whatever is true, noble, good and lovely, and there is a real need for wholesome images to be fed into our society. In our broken state, symbols of fatherhood, motherhood, family, masculinity, femininity, sonship and daughtership have become diseased symbols that fill the void. The result is that Christian symbols of God the Father, God the Son and God the Holy Spirit have also died. The prophetic artist needs to address the negative images found in society and replace them with wholesome images that can be like the 'leaves . . . for the healing of the nations' (Revelation 22:2).

Art's ability to address the full range of human emotions makes it highly effective in ministering to pain. Art can give pain a story, allowing those in pain to make sense of their suffering. So many people in our society are in need of healing, but they just do not know where to turn. The prophetic artist can show them a way out of their pain.

One aspect of the calling of the prophetic artist is to take up the role of priest. This role is to lead the people into the very presence of the Father. Where evangelism and the pastoral ministry deal with a lateral relationship between different people, prophetic priests are first and foremost in a vertical relationship with God, lifting their heads always to the Father, and encouraging others to do the same.

The prophetic artist, by changing the way people see, desires to remove the veil from people's eyes so that they can see God face to face. There is an emphasis on intimacy with God, which is vital in the life of the prophetic artist, for it is out of this place of intimacy that all true prophetic images flow. Once the prophetic artist has had a revelation from God, he or she seeks to translate it into a visual form that can communicate with the hearts of the viewers and encourage them to draw closer to God.

The viewers may not even know that it is God to whom they are responding, and here lies the power of visual representation. It cannot be easily marginalized as 'Christian propaganda', because the response is on a deep level in the secret places of the heart, where the prejudices of the mind cannot infiltrate. The prophetic artist, as we have seen, seeks to remove the veil from people's eyes. Once this is done, those people can be led to God, to look upon the face of the Father.

Prophetic artists are also called to another quite distinct role in society – that of watchmen. They are called to watch for what God is doing in the world, to read the signs and communicate what they see through relevant images. They will always be one step ahead, aware of the fact that God works through history and is working behind the scenes to unfold his sovereign plan for the redemption of the world. The watchmen are called to rebuild the city walls, speak to the world and shed light on the darkness of people's understandings. The church is seeking to reclaim the city of God here on earth, but the enemy has another agenda, and seeks to distract the troops and attack in the night when we are unaware. That is why prophetic artists are so needed – to draw attention to the danger and reality of all the enemy's cunning plans of destruction.

Prophetic artists are called to set their hands to work to restore meaning to a society plagued with meaninglessness and despair. They are called to shed light on darkened understandings, lies and deception, to illuminate people's hearts and minds in those dark places that do not know God, to depict aspects of his character. It is probably not necessary to paint a literal face of Jesus Christ, as art can show people aspects of God's nature and stir their hearts to respond. This can take many forms. A beautiful land-scape, although not necessarily Christian, can alert us to the majesty of God's creation with a wonder that seeks to understand how it all came about.

The miraculous thing about art is that it can speak numerous unrelated things to different people. The artist may physically make the image, but it is up to God to use it. A God-inspired painting does not have something phys-ically present in it. An X-ray scan would not reveal a spe-cial ingredient. It is merely an empty vessel that the Holy Spirit fills with his presence. God the Father has ordained that the Spirit will do this. Since the Spirit is living and active, he will use it purely as an interface, and will meet people in many different ways, on a personal, one-to-one level.

The calling of the prophetic artist

Bezalel was chosen by the Lord for the artistic work and designs needed for the Tabernacle. He was the first person recorded as being filled with the Spirit: 'And I have filled him with the Spirit of God, with skill, ability and knowl-edge in all kinds of crafts' (Exodus 31:3). His gifts included work in gold, silver, stone, wood, embroidery, weaving and engraving. Above and beyond his natural talents, he was specially filled with the Spirit of God so that he could do his work fully to the glory of God. Such special filling was rare in Old Testament times, so the spiritual signifi-cance and importance of this must be emphasized.

God is interested in using artists who can produce work that is so exquisite as to bring glory to him. Excellence is highly esteemed by God and there is no room in his kingdom for shoddy workers. Sadly, the church is often guilty of doing a second-rate job, cutting corners with cost and effort in a kind of embarrassment about distracting from the focus of worship. Nonetheless, the principle still remains: highly skilled work gives glory to God.

Johann Sebastian Bach wrote an average of one masterpiece a week, and yet in his striving for excellence, he did not forget that God was the source of all inspiration. He started each musical composition with the letters *J.J.*, the Latin initials for the prayer 'Jesus help me', and ended his compositions with *S.D.G.*, the initials for *Soli Deo Gloria*, meaning 'to the glory of God alone'. As Christians, we have access to the inspiration of the same God who created the universe. We should therefore strive to be excellent in all that we do, and uncompromising in our standards.

There is a great cost that comes with the calling of a prophetic artist, and it is not something to be taken on lightly. Everything you cling to that is not of God will be taken away from you, until you realize that God is all you have in this world. Until you realize that you will never be at home on earth, God will be unable to use you as a prophetic artist. This involves a great deal of self-surrender, a breaking of the will, and pain. In all of this, sensitivity to the voice of God is vital.

Knowing how to hear God's voice is so important because the prophetic artist will then be able to follow the Lord as he leads step by step. The process is always one of delving into the unknown, not knowing the full picture at the beginning. The Holy Spirit's inspiration will lead you to places where you have not been before. It is a pilgrimage – a journey with no map of start and finish, but rather signposts along the way that tell you what you need to know little by little. This cultivates a reliance on the Holy Spirit and prevents self-sufficiency. It is the Lord's way of not allowing our carnal natures – which think we are fine on our own – to take over.

How can the prophetic artist bring a message of hope unless it is totally and utterly conceived from the Lord's lips? Prophetic painting involves the act of taking up one's cross and dying to self. It does not provide a vent for self-expression, but rather for self-forgetfulness. Our minds may be aware of our own preoccupations and problems, but our spirits should be full of the presence of the Lord. We are called to be vessels that are empty enough for the Lord to fill us with his glory.

An immense fragility comes with this calling. Prophetic artists are like a flame burning in the darkness, and all people seeking after the light will be drawn to what they have to say. At the same time, the flame flickers in the wind. Prophetic artists cannot maintain that fire without the Spirit fanning it. The anointing is not something that can be controlled; it is a sovereign appointment.

11

Handling Disappointment

For we know in part and we prophesy in part.
(1 Corinthians 13:9)

Dealing with disappointments

Over a number of years the Lord has shown me some of
the visitations that he has planned. I have mentioned
already that before the establishment of Soul Survivor I
was invited to speak at a youth meeting at New Wine,
which would become Soul Survivor the following year.

I began that particular evening by leading the adults in
the main conference hall and then, having introduced the
speaker, I slipped out to walk to the youth marquee. It was
a strange evening, as there were thousands of people on
the site but they were all gathered in their respective meeting places and the area looked quite deserted.

As I walked on to the youth tent, I could hear the laugh-
ter and shouting from the children's pavilion mingled with
the songs of the young people. Outside I was alone but
then, unexpectedly in a vision, I started to see a great number of young people making their way towards the youth
pavilion. Many were running towards it, and I realized

that some were from the Scandinavian countries, others from southern Europe and the Americas, and groups soon followed from Eastern Europe, Asia and Australasia.

God was showing me that what was happening right then in the youth pavilion would be instrumental in gathering together the youth of the nations. I also sensed that the coming move of the Holy Spirit, of which this was a part, would have a strong prophetic element.

I have always enjoyed the vitality and enthusiasm of young people and was thrilled at what I saw the Lord was about to do. I knew that this generation – if encouraged and given the freedom – would fulfil God's original purpose and be a prophetic people.

During this conference a mature prophetic woman, who knew nothing of what I had seen, sought me out. She said that God was about to do a new thing prophetically with the youth, and I was to be involved in its leadership. Sadly, that was never to be.

On another occasion Mike Pilavachi and Matt Redman, the two Soul Survivor leaders, invited Mary and myself to pray for and dedicate their new premises in Watford. Soul Survivor had purchased an old warehouse on an industrial estate. This large facility had been vacant for some while and was in great need of renovation. As I walked into the derelict building I sensed that God had his hand upon this most unlikely of buildings. Together we walked around it, and I remember thinking that there was so much potential in the place.

We came into what was to become the main auditorium and worship space, and Mike asked me to pray. Suddenly everything around me was transformed. In the vision I saw hundreds of young people entering the building, and they came into an incredible time of worship. Then the scene changed, and from the building the same young people were going out in teams to the nations of the world with the good news about Jesus. Tears filled my eyes and I stood sobbing as I watched with amazement what God was doing.

At home that evening I thought how wonderful it would be to be involved in such a great work of the Spirit. This never happened. After the renovation and opening, I was invited once to speak at a meeting there, and that was my only contact.

There have been a number of similar occasions, similar disappointments, and I have come to see that the ministry of the prophet can be quite an isolated and lonely task. It can mean dealing with the excitement of what you see and hear from God alongside the fact that you will not be personally involved in its fulfilment. At times I have wished that I had not known about the thing at all!

Another area that can be hard and frustrating at times involves the future direction of the church in which you minister. Always remember that Jesus said, 'Only in his home town and in his own house is a prophet without honour' (Matthew 13:57). Do not persuade yourself that somehow it will be different for you. There have been a number of strategic occasions when I have seen clearly God's intention for the church in which I was serving. I have shared facets of this with my fellow leaders, but because of circumstance, aspects of what I saw never became a reality.

On other occasions, a waiting period is needed to allow the leadership team and the congregation to catch up in their own time with what you are already seeing clearly. This also means living with frustration.

It is important to understand that our ministry is simply to bring the word and leave it. We are not to check up to see what the leadership is doing with it. The Lord will look after his own word to bring it to fulfilment. It seems, however, that often the deciding factor is the motivation of individuals.

Conflicting prophecies

One of the embarrassing times for any emerging prophet is when they think they have a prophetic word and speak it out in the church setting, only to find it followed by an utterance which apparently contradicts what they have just said. There are a number of biblical examples of this.

In 1 Kings 13 it is recorded that an unnamed prophet came to the Temple in Bethel. Here he met King Jeroboam, who had gone to worship. The prophet had an extraordinary revelation, which I shall quote in full. It involved a future king, who was named, and a sign which would authenticate the word. The unnamed prophet spoke these words:

> O altar, altar! This is what the LORD says: 'A son named Josiah will be born to the house of David. On you he will sacrifice the priests of the high places who now make offerings there, and human bones will be burned on you.' That same day the man of God gave a sign. 'This is the sign the LORD has declared: The altar will be split apart and the ashes on it will be poured out.'
> (1 Kings 13:2–3)

When Jeroboam heard these words he was furious. He pointed to the unnamed prophet and commanded that he be seized. As he did this, his hand was shrivelled up, the altar was split apart and its ashes were poured out just as the prophet had said.

Having healed the king's arm, the prophet was invited for a meal and to receive a gift. He declined this because the Lord had expressly told him that he was not to eat or drink water, but, having given the word, he was to return home taking a different route.

As the unnamed prophet travelled home, he met a person who is described as 'an old prophet'. The 'old prophet' invited him home to have a meal, but again he declined the invitation because the Lord had forbidden it.

In reply the 'old prophet' said that he had received a visitation from an angel of the Lord who spoke to him about the unnamed prophet. He was to bring him home for food and a night's lodgings. The unnamed prophet received this as a word from the Lord. Over the meal the 'old prophet' suddenly had another revelation and said with authority,

> You have defied the word of the LORD and have not kept the command the LORD your God gave you. You came back and ate bread and drank water in the place where he told you not to eat or drink. Therefore your body will not be buried in the tomb of your fathers.
> (13:21–22).

Later that evening the prophet was killed by a lion.

If we are in a situation where there are conflicting prophecies, it is important that we hold on to what we believe God has revealed to us. If the unnamed prophet had stuck to what he knew God had said, there would have been no problem. If a contrary word comes, even from an angel, it is not necessarily to be accepted.

Expectations

In the Bible, people coming to the prophet expected a word from God. There are many examples of this, even from pagan people. On one occasion Ben-Hadad, king of Aram, was ill. He heard that Elisha was in the area and sent a message through Hazael, who was commanded, 'Take a gift with you and go to meet the man of God. Consult the LORD through him; ask him, "Will I recover from this illness?"' (2 Kings 8:7ff).

On another occasion the son of a middle-class lady died. She went immediately in search of the prophet Elisha. He saw her approaching and from outward signs he saw that she was in bitter distress. Nonetheless, he records, 'The LORD has hidden it from me and has not told me why' (2 Kings 4:27). The inference here is that normally he would know what the situation was that he confronted in a person's life.

When a person approaches an emerging prophet seeking advice, the prophet must believe that the Lord will provide a revelation. Whenever someone approaches me in this way I always pray, 'Lord, if I need to know something, show me.'

This continuous prayer has launched me on an incredible learning process. Once I was invited as a speaker to a conference in the Netherlands. During the conference one of the leaders asked me if I would talk with his daughter. She had been divorced and had started a new marriage. The specialists had told her that because of medical circumstances she was probably unable to have children in her new relationship.

We had coffee together with a friend's wife. On the way to our meeting, I thought I heard the Lord say, 'By the time the snows come next year, you will be carrying a baby girl.' As I spoke these words over her she was filled with joy. The previous week she had had a dream in which she had seen herself walking hand in hand with a little girl.

Now, many years later, the snows have come and gone many times and she is still without the daughter who had apparently been promised. She is still trying to come to terms with the various revelations. In such circumstances, all that can be said is that you gave what you thought you heard the Lord say.

There will be other times when a person approaches you for guidance. A young African woman asked me to pray and seek God for her. She had been sent to an English public school when she was seven and had been caught up in the system from then on. This had left her feeling abandoned and without hope. Now she had a decision to make. Should she stay on in England to further her career, or should she return to Africa?

Initially I asked Jesus to free her from the negative experiences she had received in her schooling. I did this by putting the event of the cross and all its power between her and the events that had left her feeling abandoned. Then I saw a crossroads. On the left was a path returning to Africa, while on the right was a path staying in England and pursuing her career. I knew her future lay in the right-hand path.

The problem here was one of giving direction from God. In such circumstances it is vital that we say what we feel *may* be the will of God, but also that we insist that future counsel from mature Christians should be sought before any life-changing decision is made. Those to whom we give such words must weigh them carefully.

Abnormal experiences

The lives of the prophets are scattered with bizarre experiences. Elijah is caught up in a whirlwind. He also seems to be taken up on occasions by the Spirit of the Lord and put down in the most unlikely places. This also happened to Philip, the young evangelist of the early church. Ezekiel was literally raised up onto his feet by the power of the Spirit. The same Spirit also translated him from Babylon to

Jerusalem. Many prophets had the most strange, and at times terrifying, visions and dreams.

There is nothing like spiritual experiences and revelations to make a person proud and arrogant. This was Joseph's initial problem after he received his dreams, and Paul says that he was given a 'thorn in the flesh' to stop him being proud of all the revelations from God that he was receiving. The description of a personal experience is not always for the public. Often we are simply to share the word which the revelation conveys.

Giving warnings

There will be occasions when you receive revelations through dreams which, although true, do not seem to have any visible effect. A year before the Labour Party was first elected to power, I had such a dream. I saw that Tony Blair would be elected with one of the largest majorities in modern times, and that the Tories would cease to be an electable party. I also saw that with such opportunity came great responsibility. This revelation was so clear that I immediately wrote to Tony Blair, who was then the leader of the opposition. I told him the facts as I saw them and their implication for government, but there was no acknowledgement.

Again, some years ago, in a dream Mary found herself walking through Marks and Spencer. She was looking through a row of clothes when the lights went out. She groped her way out and was not able to buy anything because the electrically operated tills were not working. She then looked out of the window and across the town, and saw that the lights had gone out in many of the shops. In one or two shops, however, the lights were still blazing and as she looked at them she heard a voice say, 'Power belongs to God.'

Mary felt she should write to the chairman of Marks and Spencer telling him of the substance of her dream. He did not reply. Within a very short time, however, he was sacked and the store's trading went into a sharp decline, from which it has not yet recovered.

Both these dreams had an element of truth about them and in various ways were fulfilled. We did what we could to pass on the revelations, but as far as we know they were not acknowledged in any meaningful way. This can be another area of frustration for the emerging prophet, but the key is simply to pass on what we see and trust God with the outcome.

The prophet's role is not to judge a situation, but simply to confront that situation with the revealed word of God. This word is not up for discussion with the prophet. He or she is to give it and go.

Conclusion

In this notebook I have tried to be as frank and honest as I can be. I have shared revelations that have, over the years, proved to be of God, but I have also covered the unfulfilled and the unknown. Paul summarizes the prophet's dilemma when he says, 'We prophesy in part' (1 Corinthians 13:9), and describes it as being like a 'poor reflection' (v. 12). The time will come, with the return of Jesus, when we shall see clearly and fully, but until that time we will only have glimpses of the eternal things of God.

My prayer for you is that you will take this calling seriously and will begin the great journey of seeking to know God and to hear his word.

Other books in the Ministry Guides *series . . .*

The Evangelist's Notebook
by John Peters

John Peters believes we need to make radical changes in the way we evangelise. Why would non-Christians want to come to church if they can't understand what's going on and if we can't explain to them, in everyday language, what we believe?

The Apostle's Notebook
by Mike Breen

Interest in the apostolic ministry is increasing within many streams of Christianity. Mike Breen looks at what the Bible has to say and comes to some surprising and challenging conclusions on the role of the apostle in today's church.

The Reluctant Exorcist
by Ken Gardiner

With common sense and spiritual wisdom Ken Gardiner examines such issues as distinguishing between mental disorder and demonisation, possession versus oppression, how evil spirits can gain access to individuals, including believers, and the cleansing of places.

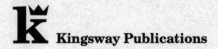 Kingsway Publications